Praise for
The Unexpected Power of Boundaries

"*The Unexpected Power of Boundaries* flips the script on everything you thought you knew about saying no. It's not about building walls—it's about creating the space you need to grow, thrive, and lead with clarity. Whether you're burned out, resentful, or just tired of people-pleasing your way through life, Sheri Jacobs offers a bold new framework for setting boundaries that feel good, do good, and make you unstoppable."

Laura Gassner Otting, *Wall Street Journal* bestselling author of *Wonderhell* and ABC contributor

"*The Unexpected Power of Boundaries* is a refreshing and essential guide for anyone navigating high-stakes leadership. Sheri Jacobs challenges the myth that innovation requires endless freedom and shows, with clarity and conviction, how real creativity thrives within smart constraints.

"I've seen Sheri speak on this topic, and she brings the same insight, energy, and practical wisdom to the page. This book will shift how you think about risk, leadership, and what it really takes to spark breakthrough ideas. A must-read for ambitious leaders and entrepreneurs ready to innovate with intention."

Shelby Meyer, Western US regional director, YPO

"I've led in combat zones, boardrooms, and bureaucracies. The same pattern shows up everywhere: people hold back when the edges aren't clear. Sheri Jacobs gets this. Her work strips away the noise and shows what actually unlocks bold thinking: boundaries that create safety, not control. If your team feels stuck or slow to act, this book gives you the tools to spot what's missing and shift it. This is for leaders who want action, not theory. It's direct, grounded, and immediately useful."

Col. (ret.) DeDe Halfhill, founder and CEO, TAIOH Partners, keynote speaker, senior executive advisor

"From the first page, Sheri dismantles myths and boldly redefines how boundaries fuel innovation. This paradigm-busting book shows leaders how to clarify chaos, unleash creativity, and build resilient, inspired teams. Read it, cling to it, and start now."

Gary LaBranche, CEO, RIMS, the risk management society

"Imagine trying to land on the moon when disaster strikes—and your only way home is to solve the impossible with what's right in front of you. That's the story of Apollo 13, and it's the same lesson Sheri Jacobs brings to *The Unexpected Power of Boundaries*: When you define the mission, set the timeframe, and work with the tools you have, you unlock focus, creativity, and results. Without boundaries, you're just floating in space."

Spencer Hulse, editorial director, *Grit Daily*

The Unexpected Power of Boundaries

Rethinking the Rules, Risks, and Real Drivers of Innovation

SHERI JACOBS

amplify
an imprint of Amplify Publishing Group

amplify
an imprint of Amplify Publishing Group

www.amplifypublishinggroup.com

The Unexpected Power of Boundaries: Rethinking the Rules, Risks, and Real Drivers of Innovation

For more information, please contact:
Amplify Publishing, an imprint of Amplify Publishing Group
620 Herndon Parkway, Suite 220
Herndon, VA 20170
info@amplifypublishing.com

Library of Congress Control Number: 2025921360

CPSIA Code: PRV1125A

ISBN-13: 979-8-89138-823-9

Printed in the United States

For my family, Jon, Jillian, Jodie, Allan, and Debbie

Contents

FOREWORD

We often assume that creativity thrives in wide-open spaces.

But what if the opposite is true?

For decades, the popular narrative around innovation has been that freedom—total, unbounded, anything-goes freedom—is the ultimate creative force. Break the rules. Erase the lines. Toss the playbook.

But what if that's exactly what's holding us back?

In *The Unexpected Power of Boundaries*, Sheri Jacobs offers a much-needed counterpoint to this approach. With clarity, depth, and a rare mix of warmth and storytelling, she makes a compelling case that we don't need *fewer* limits—we need *better* ones. That true innovation isn't about removing all constraints. It's about understanding which ones serve us and then designing them with purpose.

This book is not a call to play it safe. It's a call to play smarter.

As someone who has spent his career launching startups, investing in bold ideas, and studying the DNA of innovation, I've seen how seductive the myth around thinking outside the box can be. Sheri turns that idea on its head. She shows that when people understand where the edges are—when they feel safe to explore and clear about what matters—they actually take *more* creative risks. They stop hesitating and start experimenting.

What makes this book powerful isn't just the message—it's how Sheri delivers it. She's been in the trenches. Her stories span industries and continents, from frozen decks of Arctic expeditions to boardrooms filled with competing agendas. She's worked with everyone from early-stage startups to global associations to legacy brands trying to find their way forward. And in each case, she uncovers the same truth: People do their best work not in the absence of rules, but in the presence of the *right* ones.

As a jazz musician, I know this intimately. Jazz may sound spontaneous, but it's never random. Behind every solo is a shared structure: the chord progression, the form, the groove. These aren't constraints—they're the backbone. They give musicians the framework to take creative risks, to improvise, to explore. That's where the magic happens. Because when you know the boundaries, you can stretch them with purpose. Sheri's work brings that same spirit to the business world. She shows that when teams have structure and safety, they don't just follow the script—they riff, they experiment, and they create something unforgettable.

Sheri doesn't just illuminate this idea—she equips you to lead it. From the way meetings are structured to how feedback is framed, from evaluating risk capacity to defining the edges of innovation, this book offers concrete tools that will help you rewire how your organization works. And the best part? You won't need to blow anything up. You just need to rethink what's already there.

If you lead a team, this book will help you unlock their voice. If you run a business, this book will help you find clarity in complexity. If you've ever felt stuck trying to do something new, it will show you how to take more shots—without taking reckless ones.

This is not a book you'll read and forget. Because whether you're navigating the unknown, rolling out a bold idea, or trying to get your team to think differently, one thing is clear: The path forward isn't about unlimited freedom to explore. It's about clearer boundaries around the playground.

—Josh Linkner

New York Times Bestselling Author

Entrepreneur | Innovation Expert | Professional Jazz Guitarist

INTRODUCTION

When my daughter, Jillian, was growing up, our backyard opened right onto a municipal park. Technically, there were "boundaries"—a few burning bushes and one large oak tree—but the park really felt like an extension of our home. We often referred to it as our own "back forty" acres. The kind of place where you could run from the back porch door to the public swings without ever crossing a street or opening a gate.

For us, this was much more than a patch of grass with play equipment. It was where we spent our afternoons after work and school. I loved my job at the Association Forum, where I served as the chief membership and marketing officer, but my favorite part of the day came after dinner and before Jillian went to bed. That's when I'd open the porch screen door and watch her dash off to the playground, the sun glinting in her hair as she rushed to grab a swing before the other kids in the neighborhood.

This small park couldn't have been more simple: a large, manicured lawn housing one classic playground—swings, a slide, and an old metal merry-go-round over wood chips—plus a single sidewalk extending from one end of the park to the other. We adults would stand on one side of the playground, keeping an eye on our kids as we chatted.

Notably, no fence surrounded the park, only open, grassy fields—which you might expect to be overrun with kids throwing Frisbees, kicking soccer balls, or flying kites or drones. Oddly, this wasn't the case at all.

Even though they could technically run anywhere, our kids barely veered off the wood chips lining the play equipment. They always stayed close to us. I don't recall a single incident when someone had to chase down a child who'd wandered off.

I didn't think much about this fact until years later, when I heard about a study conducted by Tatiana Zakharova-Goodman,[1] a landscape architect with a deep curiosity about how design shapes behavior. Specifically, how kids interact with perceived boundaries in public spaces.

While earning her master's in landscape architecture, Zakharova-Goodman studied how physical environments shape children's play. She wasn't just trying to design parks that looked nice and inviting. She wanted to understand the psychology of space, especially how boundaries might influence creativity, confidence, and exploration.

So, she designed a simple experiment.

She asked a group of preschool teachers to bring their students to a local park with a small playground. This was a typical park—slides, swings, monkey bars. Just like our former "back forty" playground, this one was carpeted with wood chips and ringed on all sides by a large, grassy field stretching to quiet suburban streets. No fence or physical barrier. Just wide-open space.

The children were given just one rule: listen for that whistle that tells them it's time to leave.

If you've never lived on the edge of an open park or spent tons of time watching kids play in one, you might expect them to take off running. With that much freedom, that much space, you'd think they'd be everywhere. But they weren't. Just as I'd observed years ago, the kids stayed close to the play equipment. No one explored the open field. Some barely strayed more than a few feet from their teacher.

They had complete freedom, but they didn't use it.

Why?

Because without a clear physical boundary or instructions on how far they could venture, they didn't know where it was safe to play. They restricted themselves to a smaller play area than needed, despite ready access to more territory. With all the endless creative potential of a wide-open field, no spontaneous games of tag or "red light, green light" broke out. No one chased butterflies around the grass or crouched down to look for four-leafed clovers. They barely stepped foot off the wood chips that marked the boundary from cultivated playground to grassy, open . . . nothing.

The following week, Zakharova-Goodman repeated the experiment with the same group of preschool teachers and children. But this time, they went to a park with a fence. That physical barrier enclosed both the playground and the surrounding grassy area, creating a clear, obvious perimeter. And the moment those same kids arrived at the park? Many of the children immediately ran into the grass. Zakharova-Goodman observed them playing all kinds of improvised games as they explored all the way to the edge.

The fence didn't confine their play; it gave them the confidence to expand it.

When I read about this, I thought back to my own experiences. Not just of living near a fenceless park myself, but also of my own self-imposed constraints. How often had I imagined myself into invisible constraints when I'd actually had unlimited freedom? I began to realize that boundaries don't always restrict us. Many times, they set us free.

This realization prompted me to dive into research. Over the past two decades, I've read more studies, conducted a few myself, interviewed experts, and observed how the intersection of boundaries and innovation has impacted nearly half a million individuals across numerous industries and professions. I reviewed projects I'd worked on with startups, associations, and Fortune 500 companies.

What I found, after more than twenty years of working with organizations across nearly every industry, was the same dynamic, over and over again. Without clearly defined edges, creativity dwindles, exploration wanes, and everyone stays in a loop of convention. In keeping "safely" in the realm of "we've always done it this way," they fail to stretch and play. More to the point, they fail to adapt to market changes, to compete and grow—let alone pioneer the next new thing.

Leaders in situations like these often wonder why vague directives like "push the limits" keep falling flat. After decades of research, I realize that even the most creative and innovative minds need to first clearly understand the limitations and strategic priorities. Then, they need to build those nonnegotiables—whether of budget, infrastructure, or messaging—into their experimentation. Finally, they need to feel safe—both to speak up and to *mess up*.

If your team hesitates to experiment, if your strategic plans sound bold but stall in execution, and if you keep hearing the same five voices in every meeting, then this book is for you.

As leaders, we may *say* we want innovation. We write strategic plans and fill websites and job boards with claims about how our cultures embrace experimentation and "thinking outside the box." We hope the right combination of mission statements and meetings, of freedom and support, will spark our teams to create the next big breakthrough. To produce that new product or service that sets our organization apart from the rest. But unspoken rules, unclear priorities, and a lack of boundaries actually do the opposite: They keep teams playing small and safe.

When people don't know where the fences lie, they stick to what they know. They stay within predictable constructs already set up for them, complete with supervision and soft padding underneath. They try to replicate initiatives and projects that have found success before. When there's no clarity around what kind of experimentation their leaders support—even when they've been assured it's okay to try and fail—teams don't take more shots. They take fewer. Or none at all.

This all changes when the fence comes into view. When people know the strategic boundaries, understand the expectations, and feel genuinely safe to speak up, they start to explore. They try. They stretch. They get creative in ways that actually move the organization forward.

Still, innovation doesn't instantly flourish when teams understand the limits and feel safe to play. That is one essential component of the equation. But on its own, it rarely produces the fresh, new ideas leaders are searching for. That's why this book introduces what I call "bounded psychological safety," the combination of emotional trust and strategic clarity.

In other words, sometimes it helps to stop and think "inside the box" for a change. If, as a leader, you can clearly define the edges of experimentation and give creative minds free range to play (and even fail!) within those limits, you can shift organizational culture toward resourcefulness, ingenuity, and strategic impact, unlocking new levels of growth.

Innovation isn't about removing all limits; it's about designing better ones. When leaders get clear about where and why they encourage experimentation—and they create a culture where people feel safe to speak up—extraordinary ideas begin to surface. People stop hesitating and start experimenting. That's where real innovation takes root.

This isn't a book about moonshots or overnight breakthroughs. You won't find vague advice or one-size-fits-all frameworks. Instead, this book is about the small but powerful shifts leaders can make to invite bold thinking and real results.

Let's go back to that playground for a second. We see three forces at play in Zakharova-Goodman's study:

1. **Boundaries.** A simple fence gave children the sense of safety they needed to explore and the information they needed to know how far they could go.
2. **Voice.** Good boundaries explain what's expected and where—without prescribing *how*. These teachers didn't tell kids which games to play. The presence of the fence defined the playground while leaving the play itself unscripted, giving children the freedom to experiment with new games.
3. **Permission.** The children knew they wouldn't get scolded for running too far because the edge was obvious. Because they felt secure, their play became less tentative. They immediately spread out, exploring the full scope of their playground—past the constructs and into wide, green open space. Restrictions empowered them to play in new ways, without even having to ask.

Now let's translate that into the workplace.

You start with the *what*—the goal you want to accomplish. Next, you define the *where*. Those are the boundaries, those fences marking the edges of play. The rest—the *how*—you leave unscripted.

Too much open-ended freedom can feel foreign, overwhelming, or just empty. Meanwhile, limitations can unexpectedly unleash magic. As a small child, did you ever peer behind a bush or under a table—and see a small space suddenly come alive with possibility? Did you ever carve out a magic fort from couch cushions? Creating clear boundaries can change everything. That fence around the park defines the grass as more than just blank space. It creates a place for kids to not just explore but also to claim as their own. To use their creativity, their voices.

The same goes for the workplace. Voice is your culture; it reflects whether people at all levels feel seen, heard, and trusted. For years, I've talked about creating a culture where people "take more shots." But before they can do that, they have to know their limits and feel safe to speak up. Innovation naturally happens when boundaries, voice, and permission align.

That's what this book is about.

In Part One, we'll explore the unexpected power of boundaries—not as limits, but as opportunities or invitations to explore. You'll learn how to define constraints in ways that unleash creativity, create focus, and align your team's energy around what matters most. We'll look at companies and organizations that used clear constraints to unlock innovation, and you'll walk away with practical tools to do the same.

In Part Two, we'll focus on what can happen when you create space for every voice to be heard, especially the voices closest to the customer, client, patient, or member. You'll learn how to surface insight from the people often left out of the decision-making process and how those voices can become the engine of transformation.

In Part Three, we'll talk about what it means to take more shots—how to create a culture where experimentation is part of the workflow, not just a buzzword in a strategy deck. You'll learn how to build systems that support smart risk-taking, encourage micro-failures, and give your team permission to try, stretch, and adapt.

Throughout the book, you'll learn:

- How to define the boundaries that encourage bold thinking (and not just safe bets).
- How to structure meetings, teams, and messaging to invite more voices to the table.
- How to spot the subtle cues that signal fear or hesitation—and shift the culture.
- How to measure whether your team feels psychologically safe *and* strategically clear.
- How to build a workplace where people feel trusted, valued, and excited to explore new ideas.

Innovation doesn't happen because people are naturally brave. It happens because leaders build the kind of playground where people feel a sense of freedom to explore and create in new ways. Because they know not just which limits can be pushed, but also when, where, and how to unlock the hidden power of "thinking *inside* the box."

They know the rules. They trust the space. They feel invited to explore.

By the end of this book, you'll have tools to reframe your team's sandbox, invite more voices in, and finally unlock the kind of innovation you know is possible but haven't yet seen.

So—how big is your playground?

Not in budget or bandwidth. But in terms of the space you create for new thinking, new voices, and meaningful experimentation.

Let's find out how big your playground can truly be. In the first chapter, we'll start where innovation begins—not with a big idea, but within well-defined boundaries.

Part One

Boundaries

CHAPTER 1

You Can Do Anything but Not Everything

I had never felt so cold in my life. And I'm from Chicago, a city known for its brutal wind and snow and frigid winter temperatures. But this? This was something else entirely.

I was standing on the bow of a twelve-passenger ship, somewhere north of Svalbard, trying to photograph a polar bear at minus forty degrees.[1] That kind of cold doesn't just sting—it punishes. I couldn't feel my fingers. My camera battery kept dying. I was shivering so hard I could barely keep the lens steady. And yet, I kept trying.

A year earlier, I had signed up for a workshop with Daisy Gilardini, one of the most respected conservation photographers working in polar regions. I had visited Antarctica on a photography excursion the year before and wanted to complete the circle with one more trip— one more chance to capture something rare and breathtaking. Arctic wildlife was the final frontier on my photography wish list.

But Norway has strict laws: Boats must remain at least 500 meters from animals on land. That meant the only chance to get close to a polar bear was if one approached us on the pack ice voluntarily. So, we waited. For days. Drifting in a frozen stillness so vast and quiet, it felt like time had paused.

When a polar bear finally appeared, the call went out across the ship. It was *go time*. I put on five layers, topped by a windproof, waterproof down jacket. Daisy pulled me aside and said I needed to ditch my heated gloves; I wouldn't be able to press the shutter otherwise. So, I improvised: I shoved my fingers into a pair of cutoff heavy wool socks and hoped adrenaline would compensate for my lack of preparation and common sense.

It didn't.

My fingers went numb fast. Like frostbite fast. I took over nine hundred frames in under an hour, pretty sure that none of them would be usable. When I looked through the lens, the images looked soft, shaky.

I could feel it in my gut; I didn't get the shot. I stepped away from the deck, numb in more ways than one, as the tears began to flow down my cheeks. I felt defeated. Like I had failed at something I'd poured so much into.

Over the next few days, I tried to regroup. A crew member lent me better gloves and a warmer coat. But emotionally, I was stuck in a loop of what I didn't have: longer lenses, more experience in Arctic conditions, an understanding of how to stay warm and capture a photo of the polar bear amid the ice. My mind fixated on everything that *wasn't* available to me.

Then, on the final day of the trip, we spotted a mother walrus and her pup resting on a floating sheet of ice, framed by a soft sunset and jagged mountain peaks. It was the kind of moment you imagine before you ever book a trip like this. I carefully climbed down the icy ladder to the lower deck, trying to find a spot among a dozen others already jockeying for the best position. I had the warm clothes this time but still not the right lens. Again, I could feel it deep down. I didn't get a good shot.

The next day, when we were going through our favorite images from the workshop, Remi, one of the other members of the photography workshop, showed us a photo she'd taken earlier the previous day. It stopped me in my tracks.

It was the same walrus and pup, but from a completely different angle, taken from the top of the ship, after most of us had descended. The composition was stunning: minimal, quiet, expansive. It was the kind of photo that doesn't just show you something; it makes you *feel* it.

Here's the thing: Remi didn't have a long lens either. She also didn't have the best vantage point. She had actually injured her leg earlier in the trip and couldn't move around like the rest of us. But she had something else: clarity. She didn't spend her time lamenting what she *didn't* have. She looked around and asked, "What can I do with what I've got?" And she made something beautiful with it.

That was the moment it hit me.

I talk a lot about innovation, about working within boundaries and how limits can lead to breakthroughs. But when I was in it, when the stakes were personal, I didn't take my own advice.

This story is one I plan to revisit. Not just because I still want that perfect polar bear photo, but because it's a reminder we all need to hear—that boundaries aren't always barriers. In fact, they can be liberating. And sometimes, the most beautiful thing we'll ever make comes not in spite of limitations but because of them. Not from thinking "outside the box" but from embracing the focus and clarity that come from well-defined priorities, goals, and even essential constraints.

I've read many books promoting the idea that to lead innovative teams and differentiate your products and services, you need to give those teams more freedom. Freedom to create. Freedom to explore new ideas. Freedom to push the boundaries.

But here's the thing they miss, the thing I've seen time and time again: Without clear boundaries, people tend to play it safe. What's more, once they find a winning strategy, they are extremely unlikely to change the model. Without ongoing iteration and innovation, even those first-to-market industry leaders will fall behind.

Too often, a company's best and brightest aren't trying to experiment or innovate; they are simply trying to not get fired. They're not trying to push the limits. They just want to get through the day, without "rocking the boat" or "getting in trouble."

As leaders, we need to understand this. I've observed that most teams comprise a mix of risk-takers and rule followers. If we want our teams to innovate, we must strike a balance between "freedom" and constraints. Even some natural innovators need to understand the requirements and parameters of their jobs before they feel comfortable letting loose.

Most larger organizations have two competing divisions that create a push-pull effect when it comes to innovation. One department may work in risk management, compliance, legal, or finance. Their job is to minimize the risks and consider the material consequences of actions taken to change the company's products or policies. Another division may be focused on innovating, serving customers, and competing with other companies for market share. Without differentiating the company or iterating the product to meet changing market needs, they will lose sales. This is where establishing clear boundaries can make all the difference.

Drawing from examples across diverse industries, in this chapter, I'll show how organizations don't achieve greatness by pursuing every opportunity, but rather by creating strategic constraints that unleash creativity and drive exceptional results. When teams understand the limits of their playground, they get more resourceful and inventive. When they embrace the sandbox they have, they can really start building.

You Can Do Anything but Not Everything

Close to the end of 2019, just months before a global pandemic would force nearly every in-person meeting to go virtual, I was putting together the deck for an upcoming presentation when my former colleague, Elena Gerstmann, now executive director of the Institute for Operations Research and the Management Sciences, said these seven words: "You can do anything but not everything."

Her words have grown like a seed in my mind ever since.

This deceptively simple statement summarizes one of the most challenging aspects of leadership: making tough choices among competing priorities. When you are the one that needs to turn a plan into action, it can be difficult to focus amid the constant noise coming from multiple stakeholders, each with their own values, opinions, interests, and priorities.

Elena knows quite a lot about that. In addition to co-founding the nonprofit SocialOffset, she has served in numerous consulting, advisory, and leadership roles, including executive positions at the world's largest engineering association, the Institute of Electrical and Electronics Engineers. Through it all, Elena learned that resources may be limited, but opinions never are. They come at you from board members, investors, other C-suite leaders, employees, members, business partners, and customers.

As a leader, Elena's job—and *your* job—is to strategically select what your organization will prioritize among all these competing goals and vantage points and to effectively communicate those priorities to your team.

I thought of Elena's words as I prepared to facilitate a strategic planning meeting for a healthcare organization. Their board of directors had spent considerable time creating a clear mission and vision that persuasively expressed their purpose, but they struggled to translate this broader purpose into actionable priorities.

Their CEO, an association executive with more than two decades of leadership experience, shared that her board of directors had very passionate and well-intended opinions about where the organization should focus its attention. Each one of these diverse perspectives offered something unique and valuable. However, rather than leading to a constructive exchange of ideas, when taken together, they just seemed to stir up competition and tension.

Each director had their own pet project, my client confided to me. These board members hailed from different backgrounds—clinical, administrative, academic—and each one brought valid perspectives. But in trying to accommodate all of these viewpoints, they ended up with a "strategic" plan that lacked strategic focus. The result of this ambiguity was an unwieldy three-year plan with thirty-five loosely related objectives distributed across seven broad goals. It was more a wish list than a strategy that could serve as an actionable blueprint to guide her team.

The lack of clarity around where employees should focus attention created silos and unintended competition rather than collaboration. This led to stalled and unfinished projects, not to mention burnout, as employees felt stretched thin, demoralized, and uncertain where to spend their time. This was a classic example of attempts to "think outside the box" that only scattered sand, diminishing both resources and creative potential.

As one director shared, a team would get excited about starting an initiative only for another priority to come along and shift resources "so fast it felt like whiplash." The CEO hoped I could facilitate a discussion that would lead to narrowing their priorities and identifying stronger, more strategically aligned organizational goals.

Through interviews with her team, I learned about initiatives launched in the previous year only to be deferred or abandoned as competing priorities surfaced. Though the CEO recognized they needed to concentrate on no more than three foundational priorities to build momentum, the organization remained trapped in a cycle of dispersed efforts. They had sufficient financial resources to execute on a few projects, but they couldn't do it all. In other words, if they really put their heads together and focused their vision in a strategic, collaborative way, they could do anything . . . just not, you know, *everything*.

This organization had fallen into what I call the "abundance trap." Having too many opportunities without enough limits, guidelines, or clear directions tends to overwhelm and paralyze teams instead of empowering them to achieve their goals. By attempting to meet the demands and interests of everyone and assigning equal priority to every idea, they had created an unsustainable operation where progress was undermined by the constant pull of competing demands.

This example points out two critical components around innovation:

1. Setting constraints can be liberating instead of limiting.
2. Success comes not just from what you choose to do, but also—and equally—from what you deliberately choose not to do.

The organization's challenge wasn't a lack of capacity, resources, or talent. The CEO was confident they had a creative, skilled, and motivated team; sufficient financial resources; and, most importantly, services and resources highly valued by the market. What they lacked was focus and the strategic boundaries that would allow them to channel their resources toward meaningful impact, rather than scattering them across too many disjointed initiatives.

To help this organization establish a focused set of priorities, I developed a survey for the board of directors to complete prior to our first in-person meeting. I wanted them to independently weigh in on the issues their organization must discuss while also identifying the ones that would be nice to discuss but are no longer relevant. Next,

I asked them to select up to five trends they believed would have the greatest impact on the organization's ability to fulfill its mission. Finally, they were asked to select one—and only one—top priority from their list. The findings were enlightening.

Prior to our meeting, I shared the results with the CEO and board of directors. While the survey revealed a long, scattered list of important trends, it also showed a much greater consensus on which ones seemed most impactful to the mission and needed to be addressed first. Armed with this data, we were prepared for the first step of strategic planning: identifying the three primary focus areas. These leaders could now quickly and confidently identify which topics were essential to discuss during our strategic meeting, and which could be placed on the back burner for the time being.

The result? A new strategic plan that was feasible and would have the desired impact. The CEO's team no longer competed with each other for resources but worked collaboratively toward their goals. Because the strategy session took place just before the country went into pandemic lockdown, the organization could pivot easily while keeping their focus on a smaller set of priorities. They emerged from the pandemic stronger than their counterparts and now use this framework to guide their future planning.

Just as this healthcare organization found power in narrowing its focus, another industry—one built on storytelling—has recently embraced reinvention by drawing new boundaries around its identity and future: Cinema United.

Theaters, Boundaries, and Reinvention

On March 18, 2025, the National Association of Theatre Owners announced a rebranding: It would now be called Cinema United. The change was more than a refresh of a brand. The old name had long caused confusion due to the fact that both they and the North Atlantic Treaty Organization previously used the same acronym: NATO. But beyond avoiding misdirected emails and other cases of administrative mistaken identity, the new name signaled a renewed focus on the future of moviegoing.

This rebranding set the stage for my conversation with Lou DiGioia, Cinema United's chief operating officer. Lou oversees everything from finance and human resources to strategic planning and membership for the association. But what makes his perspective especially compelling is his boundless love of movies, something he shared with his parents growing up and now with his son. His favorite? *Avengers: Endgame*. Not only because of the story it told, but because of what it represented.

"I saw all those Marvel movies with my son," he told me. "We took a day off, watched *Infinity War* and then *Endgame* with dinner in between. It was one of the best days of my life."

I share this story because Lou's passion for the communal experience of moviegoing is woven into the very fabric of Cinema United's mission. It's not just about the movies but about the *experience* of moviegoing: the sounds, the smells of popcorn and candy, and the collective gasps in the theater. This sensory-rich community experience has been tested in recent years with the advent of streaming platforms and new content creators.

"The boundaries are real," Lou said. "And they've changed everything."

Constraints to Consider

- **Supply.** There are fewer wide-release movies than there used to be—down about 20 percent from pre-pandemic levels. If studios don't produce enough content, theaters can't fill seats.

- **Timing and competition.** Theatrical windows have shrunk. A film might go from theater to streaming in thirty days or less. Viewers now ask, "Why go now when I can just wait?" That erodes urgency—and attendance.
- **Financial pressure.** From pandemic shutdowns to production strikes, the industry has taken hit after hit. The result? A disrupted pipeline, tighter margins, and fewer resources to work with.

When movie theaters were forced to rethink their business model of how people "experienced" a movie—in other words, when the old playbook stopped working—they started to rewrite the rules. Knowing they couldn't compete with streaming platforms for price or convenience, they accepted their market limitations and instead focused on what they *could* offer. They created an *experience* that would make people want to get off the couch and go to the theater.

In a twenty-four-page report produced by Cinema United, called *The Next Great Era of Cinema*,[2] the organization highlights how their members are transforming challenges into opportunities. The strategies fell into the following three buckets.

Potential Breakthrough Boundaries

1. **Community engagement.** Some theaters now host "Knitting Night at the Movies." Others offer sensory-friendly screenings for families with neurodivergent children or bring in directors for live Q&As after the credits roll. At Spotlight Theater in Warsaw, New York, the team has created a welcoming space for local families, especially those with special needs. "We believe a movie theatre should be more than just a place to watch films—it should be a gathering space that strengthens the community," said CEO Tami Treutlein.[3]

2. **Experience upgrades.** If you've experienced a movie from a recliner that vibrates, shifts, and blows wind in your face during an action sequence, you've probably experienced 4DX. In 2024, Regal opened the largest 4DX auditorium in the world at their Times Square location.[4] It's not just a movie. It's a multisensory ride.

    Other chains are making similar bets: installing laser projectors, expanding IMAX and HDR screens, and adding upscale food and drink options. The message is clear: "You can't get this experience at home." Rather than trying to compete on price or ease, they're drawing a bold line between streaming convenience on one hand and the cinematic immersion that now differentiates this new wave of moviegoing.

3. **Rethinking the space.** Some theaters are becoming part amusement park, part art house, and part community center. One chain added bowling alleys, bars, and even a (literal) playground so families come early, let their kids play, and then head into the movie together. Another theater replaced seats with beds in one of its rooms. Not beanbags. Actual beds.

    At the Southampton Playhouse, which reopened in 2025 as a nonprofit, the innovation is cultural. They pair eclectic programming—everything from international indies to classic film retrospectives—with thoughtful touches like post-film workshops, lectures, and a weekly email from their artistic director blending journalism with film history. Beyond typical moviegoing, patrons now enter a whole experience ecosystem.[5]

    Thinking *inside* a (reimagined) sandbox like this can bring everything together: community, experience, and story. As I write this, Marcus Theatres have already hosted three sold-out star-studded premieres, including one for *The Unbreakable Boy*, the real-life story of a Marcus associate and his family. They turned the local cinema into something much more than a venue. It became a stage for community, collaboration, and connection.

These aren't the kinds of ideas you implement when everything is going smoothly. They're born out of necessity, constraints that demand some improvisation and innovation.

Lou shared a key question facing theaters today: "If the movies aren't coming, what can we show?" The answers range from repertory films to faith-based blockbusters to community-curated content. "Angel Studios had a huge hit with *King of Kings*. It brought in nearly $20 million," he says. "That kind of success comes from looking at the boundary and saying, 'What's possible inside it?'"

However, like most companies that strive to innovate, not everything worked. One well-documented failure occurred when AMC tried charging more for premium middle seats—an airline-style model. It didn't go over well. Customers pushed back, and the company reversed course. But Lou doesn't see it as a failure.

"Maybe it was the framing," he told me. "If this concept was framed as, 'discount pricing for front row seats,' instead of, 'premium for the middle,' people might've seen it differently."

He pointed out another experiment that has worked: Discount Tuesdays. "It far outperforms midweek days like Monday or Wednesday," Lou said. "Someone's going to crack tiered pricing by day of week. It's just a matter of time."

And it's not just pricing. Theaters are adapting to an entirely new landscape, one where a streaming platform like Netflix can loom large, while still operating within their own self-imposed constraints. Because while Amazon and Apple have embraced theatrical releases, Netflix continues to hold back. And as we'll see in the next section, this isn't the only strategic constraint that's helped Netflix focus its efforts and dominate streaming.

"Netflix's best-performing content often had a theatrical window and ended up on their platform," Lou said.

Throughout our conversation, one message rang clear: The boundaries theaters face aren't just roadblocks; they're proving grounds. The limitations around content, time, and budget are pushing theater owners to explore new ideas, redesign their spaces, connect with communities, and question assumptions.

That's the power of boundaries. Not as barriers, but as frames that focus us. They provide the boundaries of the space so creative teams can create something unforgettable.

The story of AMC's pricing experiment shows how quickly customers push back when a boundary feels arbitrary or poorly framed. It also reveals something deeper: the power of perception. A small shift from "charging more" to "discounting differently" might have changed the entire narrative, as well as the company's bottom line. That kind of boundary-setting isn't just about limiting options; it's about guiding focus. And, as we'll explore next, no company has mastered that balancing act better than Netflix.

Key Takeaways

1. **Constraints create clarity.** When the usual supply of blockbuster films dried up, theaters didn't sit back and wait. They started asking new questions: *What can we offer that can't be found elsewhere? Who are we serving?* Regardless of your industry, scarcity can sharpen your focus. Boundaries, like tighter budgets or fewer resources, force teams to prioritize what matters and stop chasing everything.

2. **Experience can differentiate.** Cinema United members didn't try to compete with streaming platforms on convenience.

Instead, they leaned into what only they could offer: immersive formats, sensory-rich environments, and a shared experience.

3. **Community is a strategy.** From sensory-friendly screenings to curated local events, theaters are redefining their value as community hubs. Know who you serve and serve them in ways that are personal, meaningful, and unexpected. When you create space for people to gather, share, or feel seen, you build more than a customer base. You build loyalty.

How Netflix Uses Boundaries to Drive Innovation

As theaters leaned into what made their experience irreplaceable, Netflix took a different approach. It drew its own set of boundaries— not around place, but around purpose. It used these boundaries to fuel one of the biggest reinventions in entertainment history. Under the leadership of CEO Reed Hastings and Chief Content Officer Ted Sarandos, Netflix established a culture that balances creative freedom with clear strategic parameters.

Most references to Netflix's culture focus on its well-known lack of traditional constraints—no vacation policies, no expense approval processes, and minimal organizational hierarchy. But this freedom exists within a carefully constructed framework of strategic boundaries that redirect creativity toward creating and distributing content that stands out in a crowded market.

This culture of creative thinking "inside the box" helped Netflix pivot from streaming the content of other studios to becoming one of the most innovative content creators in the world. In 2011, Netflix had approximately twenty-three million subscribers and was primarily known as a streaming platform. But executives knew their business model would soon face some major challenges. First, as Netflix grew, outside studios increased the fees to license and stream their content.

Second, several networks and studios were in the process of building their own streaming services and threatened to pull their content from Netflix.

Ted Sarandos and Reed Hastings knew they needed to differentiate themselves if they wanted to thrive in the future. So, they made the pivotal decision to invest in original programming. As Sarandos put it at the time, "The goal is to become HBO faster than HBO can become us."[6]

But Netflix didn't try to "boil the sea" and appeal to everyone when it came to developing new shows. Instead, they incorporated strategic content constraints. One of these most critical constraints involved portfolio boundaries. Netflix balances investments aimed at established genres and formats with proven audience appeal, emerging areas that show promise, and experimental content that might establish new categories. While Netflix invests more in established genres, they also understand the immense advantage they've gained from collecting viewer data.

Unlike traditional movies, Netflix knows what viewers watch, when they pause, when they rewind, and when they abandon shows altogether. They know which actors and directors garner the highest interest among various audience segments, which genres appeal to various audience segments, and how large the audience segment's potential may be. Netflix uses this data and its investment strategy to create clear parameters for producing new content while still allowing for significant innovation within each category. Directors of established romantic comedies know they have different success metrics than creators of experimental documentary formats. These boundaries create clarity around expectations and freedom to explore within appropriate parameters—often leading to breakthroughs.

For Netflix, these breakthrough boundaries became formalized as part of the creative process. They fall into three main categories:

1. Taste communities
2. Minimum viable audience
3. Clear feedback boundaries

Taste Communities

Rather than trying to please everyone, an approach many Hollywood studios take when producing movies, Netflix created thousands of "taste communities"—groups of viewers with similar watching behaviors regardless of age, gender, or location.[7] These communities serve as essential creative parameters, giving creators a clearly defined audience to satisfy rather than trying to appeal to the generic masses.

This approach led to the commercial and critical success of their 2020 series *The Queen's Gambit.* To develop this show, the creative team analyzed data collected from millions of subscribers worldwide about a specific taste community: one that enjoyed character-driven dramas with strong female leads and distinctive visual storytelling. They weren't told what show to make, but they had clear boundaries around the audience they were making it for. *The Queen's Gambit*, based on Walter Tevis's 1983 novel by the same name, fit these constraints. The show follows the fictional protagonist, Beth Harmon, an orphan who becomes a chess prodigy during the Cold War era. Beth navigates the male-dominated world of elite competitive chess while struggling with an addiction to tranquilizers and alcohol. The show became one of Netflix's highest-rated and most-watched series. It also won eleven Emmy Awards during its run, including Outstanding Limited Series.[8]

According to one estimate I read, Netflix has defined parameters around more than 1,300 taste communities.[9] These content limitations help company creatives focus on yet another strategic boundary: Netflix's minimum standards for creating a new show.

"Minimum Viable Audience" as a Boundary

In contrast to traditional networks, which often cancel shows that don't achieve a standard level of viewership (especially from key demographic audiences), Netflix employs a "minimum viable audience" approach. They determine upfront the audience size a particular show needs to reach to justify its cost. Next, they evaluate success against that specific benchmark, rather than comparing all shows to some universal standard.

This creates boundaries that liberate creators. As Ted Sarandos put it, "We look at it on a case-by-case basis, in terms of how a film or series performs against the expectations that we had for it . . . some are for massive audiences; some are for very specific audiences. And all we need to do is size the investment to the size of the audience."[10] Netflix doesn't need everything to be a home run. Some content is meant for tens of millions of viewers, and some is meant for a passionate million. Netflix sees success in both situations, each on their own terms.

Clear Feedback Boundaries

Perhaps most importantly, Netflix leaders established clear boundaries around how and when they give feedback to creative teams. Rather than the traditional model of constant executive notes (or, as many people involved in the creative process call it, "interference"), Netflix provides comprehensive feedback only during the initial development phase. After that, they allow creators full autonomy during production.

Shonda Rhimes, executive producer of *Bridgerton*, once described this bounded approach as "liberating," compared to her experience at traditional networks: "The first thing I said was, 'You're not going to tell me when my shows have to end or how long they have to be?' And he said, 'Nope.' I said, 'I'm going to make what I want to make?' And he said, 'Yes.' I said, 'The budgets are going to be what I think they should be?' And he said, 'Yes.' The answer was always just, 'Yes, yes, yes.'" [11]

Netflix's initial feedback includes a collaborative process and deep dive at the outset, where executives and creative teams engage in detailed discussions with clearly defined success metrics. However, unlike traditional models that drip-feed notes throughout production, often altering course midstream and effectively overriding the vision of the team creating the show, Netflix frontloads this input with clear guidelines that set fence posts around the creative playground.

After that, Netflix steps back. With guidelines clearly articulated upfront, creators like Shonda Rhimes can play unencumbered by micromanagement. They can experiment, innovate, and follow their creative instincts freely, within agreed-upon sandbox and playground constraints. The boundary Netflix sets isn't restrictive; it's empowering. By understanding where the edges lie, creators no longer waste energy anticipating objections or navigating changing expectations.

Netflix could say, "Yes, yes, yes," to Shonda Rhimes because those fences were already in place, defining, and emphasizing, how much open space they had to roam. Those strategic boundaries didn't constrain creativity; instead, they encouraged greater exploration, innovation, and creativity. First, they defined clear parameters around audiences, investment categories, success metrics. Then, they reinvented the feedback processes to create conditions for creative teams to explore more boldly . . . much like children who venture to the very edges of fenced-in playgrounds.

When boundaries are clearly identified, we gain bounded psychological freedom. We better appreciate and utilize the resources and possibilities contained within our sandboxes, rather than ineffectually scattering and dispersing them. We build more effectively. We embrace the freedom to explore all the way to the edges, experimenting in ways that we may never have before.

When I think back to my trip to the Arctic and how I could have better handled the challenges I faced in minus forty temperatures with equipment limitations, one thing stands out. Many times, the most powerful creative breakthroughs often happen inside the box, not outside of it. When we reframe success, let go of what's out of reach, and ask what's possible with what's right in front of us, everything changes.

In the next chapter, I'll present three approaches for establishing strategic boundaries that can help you minimize risk and create a culture of innovation. Together, these approaches create the conditions for organizations to excel by doing fewer things better, rather than spreading their efforts across too many priorities.

YOUR TURN TO THINK DIFFERENTLY

As you reflect on the ideas in this chapter, consider how these concepts apply within your own organization. These and other end-of-chapter questions throughout the book are designed to help you challenge assumptions, explore new boundaries, and uncover opportunities to think differently—intentionally and strategically.

1. Do you establish the same parameters for all new program or product launches, or are success measurements based on minimum viable products, opportunity, and audience size?
2. How would defining your organization's version of specific "taste communities" change your approach to product or service development?
3. What would a "minimum viable audience" look like for your most important strategic initiative?

CHAPTER 2

Rethinking Risk Capacity

There's one phrase I've heard so many times I've lost count: "We are a data-driven organization."

In our data-rich work environments filled with easy-to-use online survey tools and customer relationship management systems, organizations now collect extensive metrics—often without translating them into strategic, actionable parameters that guide decision-making and spark innovation. The key to success isn't just gathering data; it's transforming those facts and figures into well-defined boundaries that give teams freedom to explore within them.

These boundaries can act like guardrails—not to restrict motion, but to ensure forward movement in the right direction. They can also help you identify the boundaries that may have been in place for years but could now be moved (as we'll explore more in chapter 3). Data can clarify what's acceptable to test, where to invest resources, and when to pause or pivot. It can also uncover problems that may have been hidden or overlooked.

Too often, organizations pride themselves on being "data-driven," but that mindset can inadvertently limit their understanding of risk capacity. When every decision hinges on having complete data, teams may avoid actions that involve uncertainty, which are precisely the kind of actions that innovation requires. Risk capacity is about understanding what your organization can handle, even in the absence of full information. This shift enables faster learning, more resilience, and a greater tolerance for uncertainty.

Without that awareness, leaders either overcorrect, clinging to certainty and resisting new ideas, or they launch ambitious projects without building the internal scaffolding to support them. The results? Missed opportunities, burned-out teams, or public stumbles that erode trust.

That's why I argue for being data-*influenced* instead of data-driven. Data should inform and shape our choices but not "drive" or dictate them. The distinction may seem subtle, but it's actually quite profound. A data-influenced organization listens to the signals, identifies patterns, makes other voices heard, and uses all those insights to test and experiment new ideas. Data can also be used to set boundaries that protect what matters most while encouraging the kind of experimentation that leads to breakthroughs. Examples might include a minimum acceptable percentage of customer service complaints, or the amount of time it takes for an individual to engage or make a purchase. Those boundaries aren't just financial or operational; they're also emotional and cultural. And getting data-influenced boundaries in place require a deep understanding of *risk capacity*.

Risk *capacity* is different from risk *tolerance*. Tolerance is psychological. It's how comfortable a person or a team feels about change when faced with elements of uncertainty. Capacity, on the other hand, is structural. It's the actual cushion you have to make changes, experiment, and even fail. A startup might have a high psychological tolerance for risk but very low material capacity. Meanwhile, a legacy association might have plenty of resources to take more risks but remain nevertheless paralyzed by low tolerance.

In the previous chapter, I discussed how Netflix approached content development. They don't just collect viewing data; they also translate it into specific "taste communities" and engagement metrics that become creative guardrails for their content creators. The parameters they put into place don't dictate precisely which shows to make, but they do establish clear boundaries within which creative teams have freedom to innovate.

Netflix's approach to data transformation offers initial feedback and guidance, which informs each show's original content development.

Examples of Netflix Content Criteria

- **Slow-burn complexity.** "Content should appeal to viewers who enjoy 'slow burn' storytelling with morally complex characters."
- **Viewer retention.** "This series should maintain a [defined percentage] of episode-to-episode retention for its target taste community."
- **Demographic crossover.** "This comedy should drive at least a [defined minimum percentage] of viewing outside its primary demographic."

By transforming raw data into these creative boundaries, Netflix gives creators clear targets without prescribing how to hit them. This balances guidance with creative freedom.

This approach can be adapted across industries. Healthcare organizations might establish data-influenced parameters like "Solutions must provide follow-up care content within forty-eight hours," or "Develop tools that support thirty-day behavior tracking," instead of vague directives to "improve patient experience."

The Experiment That Changed Everything

Some boundaries show up in spreadsheets; others arrive in the form of silence. For SurePayroll, a company that was acquired by Paychex and became a subsidiary, serving thousands of small businesses across the country, one of its clearest early boundaries came from a single marketing experiment that helped shape its entire growth strategy. Back then, SurePayroll was a startup with a vision to bring payroll online and make it effortless for small business owners—and I happened to be working on its founding management team.

When I recently caught up with Troy Henikoff, one of SurePayroll's co-founders, he recalled a story about the startup's early collaboration with Citibank. In this example, a seemingly perfect growth campaign taught the team why defining better, data-informed boundaries upfront can be one of the most freeing and strategic things a business can do.

Back in SurePayroll's early days, the company was trying to figure out the best way to acquire customers. Because digitized, online payroll services were still in their infancy, we had built a model around direct marketing. You send four hundred mailers at a dollar apiece, get a 1 percent response rate, convert a quarter of those into customers, and you're left with one new account for every $400 spent. That was the theory.

But direct marketing wasn't performing the way we'd hoped. The response rates were inconsistent. We needed clearer data to determine if the channel was even worth continuing.

Then came the golden ticket—at least we thought so at the time. SurePayroll had an opportunity to co-brand a campaign with Citibank. The pitch was that SurePayroll would offer Citibank's small business customers a special deal: ninety days of free payroll, plus a discounted rate going forward. In return, Citibank could promote it as added value for their small business accounts, making their services stickier. It seemed perfect. Citibank had already built a strong reputation of trust with its customers. Plus, SurePayroll's service would offer a savings to small business owners.

The campaign itself seemed well-designed. We printed small slips of paper roughly the size of a dollar bill (called "buck slips" in the marketing world) and inserted these directly into three hundred thousand monthly bank statements. Each buck slip had Citibank's logo on one side, SurePayroll's on the other, and a short, clear offer: "Just call the 1-800 number listed to sign up." From a marketing perspective, it was close to perfect.

The Conventional Metrics (That Didn't Add Up)

- **100 percent delivery.** You knew the envelope would arrive.
- **100 percent open rate.** This was pre-digital banking, so everyone opened their paper statements.
- **Highly targeted.** These slips reached exactly the right people: small business owners and the decision-makers who handled payroll.
- **Instant credibility.** Citibank's brand endorsement helped build trust.

The team was ready. SurePayroll even hired temps and brought in extra phones so we could handle a deluge of calls. Henikoff remembers what happened next with mathematical precision: "We got three calls and one customer—out of 300,000 well-targeted, well-timed, co-branded offers, we landed exactly one customer."

This wasn't a marketing shot in the dark. It was a controlled test with a clear hypothesis. SurePayroll knew what "success" would look like. Just as importantly, we knew what failure would look like too.

The minute those results came in—three calls, one customer—
Henikoff pulled the plug. Right then and there. All marketing spending
stopped immediately. The ad agency was told to wrap any work already
completed, but no new work would move forward.

This was a boundary moment. The numbers were not close. They
weren't promising. In fact, they were pretty conclusive.

> Our team could have acquired more data—you know, in the
> interest of being "data-driven." We could have tested different
> offers or tweaked the wording or other campaign components.
> But we didn't have the luxury of follow-ups. We knew our most
> delicate area of risk capacity was time. SurePayroll needed to
> quickly acquire new customers during this critical early growth
> phase as a fledgling startup.

Besides, the hypothesis had been proven wrong, decisively. As
Henikoff put it, "We weren't even in the right zip code. There was no
logical argument that could justify continuing." Continuing would
have meant ignoring clear evidence in favor of misdirected hope. So,
Henikoff used the data from the experiment to influence his next move.

He didn't just walk away; he redirected. SurePayroll shifted its
focus entirely to direct sales. Yes, it was slower. And more expensive.
But it *worked*. The model was sustainable, the customers stayed longer,
and eventually the company was successfully acquired by Paychex.

It all started with a single failed experiment that was clearly
bounded by objective metrics of time. That's what real creative boundaries look like. Not arbitrary limits, but intentional lines that allow you
to move with focus, test with clarity, and let go without regret when
something doesn't work.

Without strategic limits on time and other resources, you're
not really testing. You're drifting. You're convincing yourself that

maybe—just maybe—it'll turn around next month. Too often, it doesn't.

In the world of innovation, we hear a lot about risk tolerance, but not as much about risk capacity. Understanding the difference between these two can be the key to getting your organization out of the yearslong habits and developing a new approach to innovation.

Swing Smarter, Not Harder

At the height of the 2021 pandemic lockdown, when everyone I knew was trying their hand at sourdough bread, I decided to take up tennis. I had moved from Chicago to Denver at the beginning of the pandemic, and tennis soon became my lifeline to meeting new people and forming new friendships. I joined the Denver Tennis Club and set my sights on playing in one of the USTA leagues sponsored by the club.

There was only one problem. Although I'm fairly athletic, having run eighteen marathons over the last two decades, this did not translate into instant success on the tennis court. There were many days when I came off the court, threw my racket and bag into the backseat of my car, and swore I would never play again.

However, on most days, by the time I arrived back at my house, I had shifted my mindset from *I can't do this* to *I struggle to do this*. I started working with one of the pros at the club and attended every tennis drill I could fit in with my work schedule. Then I looked at how my tennis gear—my shoes and racket—might help improve my game.

I did what any new player who wants to get better does; I bought a top-of-the line tennis racket and a pair of tennis shoes named after the great Roger Federer. As a novice tennis player, I figured I couldn't go wrong with a product named after one of my all-time favorite tennis legends.

What I failed to consider is that shoes designed for a great athlete don't guarantee great performance—nor even, in my case, *safety*. Not if you use them in the wrong way. Turns out, these "tennis shoes" weren't even designed for the court but rather intended to be leisure shoes. Sure enough, I twisted my ankle within a month of buying them. This uninformed "impulse buy" sidelined me for weeks in a not-so-gentle reminder to respect the boundaries of the game and gather additional data before making decisions.

Sometimes, feelings can fill in for lack of data. This personal misstep illustrates an important aspect of *risk capacity*: the idea that taking a risk isn't just about tolerance (i.e., how you *feel* about the idea); it's also about your resources. It requires gathering enough information to understand the limits of your own knowledge and resources, and to better understand your environment so you know what it takes to achieve your goals.

I had the willingness to try something new and an adequate tennis shoe budget, but I hadn't gathered enough data to understand my options, nor even my safety risks. I didn't seek expert advice or even ask other players about what they found to be useful—and I learned my lesson the hard way.

Which brings us to On.

The Swiss shoe company, On, built its reputation on the revolutionary "CloudTec" sole technology beloved by runners worldwide, including me. I had worn these shoes (often referred to as "On Clouds") to run seven marathons, including the Boston Marathon, a race that you need to qualify for in order to participate.

Once On had achieved moderate success in the running community, they turned their sights to tennis and formed a strategic partnership with Roger Federer. Their collaboration led to the development of the Roger Centre Court line, which debuted in July 2020 with a lifestyle sneaker and later expanded to include performance tennis shoes like Roger Pro in 2021.[1] The Roger Pro evolved from a meticulous design process that incorporated Federer's on-court knowledge and the demands of professional (or in my case, recreational) tennis. But On didn't make the leap blindly. They didn't aim to dominate tennis overnight; they aimed to learn. That's why they started with the leisure shoe, and after that hit the market, they continued to work on creating a performance shoe that could be used on the court.

When they launched the first leisure shoe, On received both enthusiastic reviews and constructive feedback (a.k.a., critical reviews). There were reports of the shoe running tighter than anticipated, which affected overall comfort for some users, according to customer reviews on the Dick's Sporting Goods website. In response, On made several adjustments in subsequent models. A later version, known as Roger Advantage, addressed comfort concerns.

Once they experienced success with the Roger Centre Court and the Roger Pro, On signed other top-ranked players, like Iga Świątek and Ben Shelton, in 2023.[2] In 2024, On partnered with actress Zendaya to bridge the gap between sport, fashion, and culture, enhancing the brand's appeal beyond traditional athletic audiences.[3] By understanding their *risk capacity*—a strong brand reputation, a loyal customer base, and trusted design technology—they could afford to take an informed risk and iterate quickly.

The result? A product line that not only appealed to both recreational and competitive tennis players but also subtly redefined what performance footwear could feel like. On didn't wait years for perfect data; they acted promptly on good-enough data. They moved from the single-use performance niche of running to a larger identity by expanding thoughtfully, one step at a time.

In innovation, just like in tennis, it's not about swinging your racket without intention; it's about choosing where you want to place your shots. Knowing when the risk is worth it, when your footing is solid, and when to pivot. My own misstep with the wrong shoes was an ankle-twisting lesson in how to approach risk. On's story is a more graceful version of the same idea: understand your constraints, test smartly, and evolve confidently.

Risk capacity isn't about how much risk you *want* to take. It's about how much risk you *can afford* to take.

Risk Tolerance ≠ Risk Capacity

Risk tolerance is about comfort levels. It's subjective and emotional, based on past experiences or personal preferences. On the other hand, risk capacity is rooted in objective material facts. It's about what your organization can actually handle, regardless of how you *feel* about it.

That's where bounded psychological safety comes in. When people feel safe to either speak up or take action *within clearly understood boundaries*, they're more likely to engage in constructive risk-taking. You're not asking people to leap off cliffs—you're helping them see where the ledge is, and how far they can stretch without falling.

To help determine a team's risk capacity, have team members rate how much they agree with each statement on a scale of 1–10, where 1 indicates strong disagreement, and 10 indicates strong agreement. Once the quiz is completed, add up the scores.

Risk Capacity Quiz	
Score 1–10	**Rate how much you agree with the following statements.**
	We have a stable and predictable revenue stream.
	Our revenue comes from multiple, diverse sources.
	Our organization maintains substantial cash reserves relative to our operating expenses.

Risk Capacity Quiz	
Score 1–10	**Rate how much you agree with the following statements.**
	We have communicated clear boundaries around what can be changed or modified.
	Our organization has a strong and positive reputation within our industry.
	Our work culture actively encourages and supports experimentation and new ways to recruit and engage members.
	We have an efficient and effective process for evaluating and implementing new ideas.
	Our organization successfully balances maintaining current operations with exploring new opportunities.
	If needed, we could quickly and effectively pivot or change direction.
	Leaders in our organization actively encourage innovation and are willing to take calculated risks on new ideas.
	10–40: **Low Risk Capacity:** Your organization should identify low-risk opportunities to experiment with before investing significant time and resources into new initiatives. 41–70: **Medium Risk Capacity:** Your organization can experiment but should carefully consider the scale and potential impact of new initiatives, along with the impact of doing nothing at all. 71–100: **High Risk Capacity:** Your organization is well-positioned to experiment and try new ideas, but it should still maintain prudent risk management practices.

Understanding your organization's risk capacity isn't just a theoretical exercise; it sets the foundation for action. When working with companies and organizations that want to innovate but view experiments as too risky, one of the biggest stumbling blocks I've observed is a lack of understanding regarding risk capacity. That's why I developed this quiz, to help leaders and teams look beyond their psychological comfort zone to gauge how much risk they can actually afford. The goal is to make more intentional decisions about where and how to experiment. It's the difference between guessing where you might push boundaries and knowing where the edge truly lies.

I've also seen organizations overestimate their capacity for experimentation or change, only to stumble from a failed initiative. Risk capacity isn't about being a fearless leader. It's about taking right-sized risks at the right time, in the right way.

Finally, risk capacity isn't static; it shifts as your revenue diversifies, as leadership evolves, and as your culture changes. That's why identifying your capacity is only the beginning. The next step is building the habits, systems, and shared language to continually navigate risk with intention. That's where discipline comes in—not as a constraint, but as a framework for creative freedom.

The Discipline of Risk

When Rob Barnes joined Betty as co-founder and CEO at the end of 2023, he wasn't stepping into a role so much as stepping into a bet. "I was the only employee at the start," Barnes told me in a personal interview. "As customers have come on board, we've grown the team."

That lean beginning shaped not only Barnes's view of leadership but also how the company approaches decision-making under pressure. They learned, out of necessity, to be disciplined about how they view risk—not just for themselves, but also for their clients and partners.

Betty is named after Betty Holberton, a pioneering computer scientist whose work left an indelible mark on the field of computing. During World War II, Holberton was one of six women selected to work on the ENIAC (which stands for "Electronic Numerical Integrator and

Computer"), the world's first general purpose electronic computer. It was mainly used to calculate ballistic trajectories.[4]

When Barnes and his colleagues developed Betty, their vision was to partner with associations to help them empower members, volunteers, and staff by providing seamless access to the knowledge they need. "My role is to stay true to our purpose, maintain focus, and make sure we're building alignment with our mission," Barnes shared with me during our conversation about Betty's origin story.

That alignment provides the boundaries needed to ground their strategy in company values, namely, supporting associations to do more connective, higher-level human work—by letting AI take care of the busywork.

"The idea is, 'Can we solve a problem with AI before involving humans?'" Barnes said. "Not to replace humans, but to free them up for high-value connection." For associations, where Betty focuses its work, those human connections are central to the business model. Barnes's approach is to let Betty handle the noise so humans can turn up the volume on what matters most.

However, there are plenty of risks involved in this intersection between the deeply human, connection-based associations and the emerging technology of AI. That's why Barnes trains his teams to be disciplined about anticipating and proactively addressing risk factors affecting their association partners.

"Associations are uniquely positioned to benefit from AI. They are massive repositories of industry knowledge, knowledge that has been curated, peer-reviewed, and refined over decades," Barnes shared. But that trust has been quietly eroded by lesser sources of generative AI, which can produce factually incorrect content that nevertheless appears credible.

Given the long-standing credibility of professional and trade associations, Barnes knew that Betty needed to match their rigorous standards and commitment to accuracy. Their mission was to make the Betty engine an extension of the trust that already exists within association communities. Unlike generic AI tools, which can produce misleading information, Barnes's team designed Betty specifically for member-based organizations by exclusively using the association's proprietary content to train the algorithm. This ensures that the information is accurate, relevant, and reflective of the organization's expertise. Betty also maintains transparency, so members can trust the source of information they receive.

As Barnes and his team built this AI tool to support associations, their guiding principle was clear: Never deliver anything that could put their partner organizations at risk. "We've defined what we can afford to mess up," Barnes explained. "We ask ourselves, 'Will this negatively affect a customer?' If so, we pull back. If not, and we can afford the financial risk, we move ahead."

What does this look like in practice? One example is the risk Betty takes on related to user engagement. The platform's operating costs are tied to usage—specifically, tokens, which fluctuate in price depending on the AI model powering the platform. As associations successfully engage more members through Betty, usage and costs increase significantly. Rather than passing those additional expenses onto the association, Barnes and his team absorb the financial impact. "Associations need predictability in their annual budgets," Barnes shared. "We don't want them to feel penalized for driving success."

Another risk the team willingly takes on is managing which AI model powers the experience. With new models emerging rapidly—each with trade-offs in speed, performance, and functionality—keeping up requires significant time and resources. "That's our job, not theirs," Barnes said. "We want association leaders focused on their mission, not comparing backend model specs. All they need to know is that Betty works, and we handle the rest behind the scenes."

This isn't recklessness. It's informed experimentation. "We talk about 'two-way doors,'" Rob explained. "You try something, and if it doesn't work, you walk back through and try something else. The key is having a hypothesis: 'I believe if we do X, it will lead to Y.' If it doesn't, fine. We still learned something."

That distinction, being data-influenced versus data-driven, is subtle but critical. At Betty, the data doesn't tell the team what actions to take. It tells the team what questions to ask. "We regularly brainstorm hypotheses: 'Wouldn't it be great if . . . ?' or 'I wonder if we could . . . ?' Then we test those." According to Barnes, that disciplined, ongoing approach to assessing risk capacity is something organizations and companies urgently need to build.

"I wish more people asked: *What will happen if we don't do this*?" he said. "That opens the door to risk management, governance, and realistic conversations." In other words, the real risk isn't trying something new. It's doing nothing at all.

Use Risk Capacity to Transform Data into Creative Boundaries

1. **Know the difference between "ready" and "willing."** One of the most common missteps in innovation strategy is confusing *willingness* to take risks with *readiness* to take them. Willingness is emotional; it's about how an individual, team, or company *feels* about risks—and it's often fueled by ambition, urgency, or fear of being left behind.

   Readiness, however, is based on real resources, like cash reserves, operational bandwidth, leadership alignment, company goals and values, and brand strength. For example, a membership association may want to launch a new dues-based membership model after seeing a significant drop in recruitment and retention, but they hesitate to do so because they're risk-adverse and therefore uncomfortable with change. Successful leaders assess risk not in terms of feelings, but rather in terms of brand reputation, material capacity for failure (including financial reserves), and past effectiveness in experimenting and iterating to understand how to best serve their communities.

2. **Look for boundaries.** Boundaries often get a bad rap, especially in creative and entrepreneurial circles. They're seen as restrictive, bureaucratic, or anti-innovation. But boundaries, when drawn from a clear understanding of risk capacity, can actually do the opposite. They provide a safe space for innovation to flourish. At SurePayroll, the marketing experiment with Citibank didn't just fail; it also helped the team draw a critical boundary: no more high-cost, low-return direct marketing partnerships. That freed them to reallocate time, money, and attention to what *did* work. Boundaries, when shaped by a clear understanding of risk capacity, are not just about saying "no"—they're about saying "yes" with intention and purpose.

3. **Assess risk capacity as part of your data-influenced strategy.** Too often, decisions about innovation, expansion, or restructuring get made in board meetings or senior staff meetings based on "instinct," experience, or who has the loudest or most persuasive voice in the room. But assessing risk capacity should instead be treated as a repeatable leadership discipline.

    This includes:

    • Scoring your organization across the ten-item Risk Capacity quiz.

- Holding quarterly "risk review" sessions that ask, *What risks are we currently taking? What did we say "no" to? What did we pause? Why?*
- Documenting the thresholds for failure in any major initiative. Asking questions like, *What does success and failure look like in advance? Do we have the capacity to fail, and how would we recover?*

When leaders regularly assess and revisit their risk capacity, they can move more decisively because they're acting from a place of structure, not speculation.

4. **Become disciplined within your risk capacity.** Medium risk capacity is the most misunderstood and possibly the most dangerous zone. Not because they're the most vulnerable, but because they mistakenly believe they are ready to go "all in." You need to build the systems, culture, and flexibility to sustain major disruption. This is where "right-size innovation" becomes critical. Even organizations with sufficient financial resources should test hypotheses by conducting small-scale pilot projects before wider market launch.

   Betty is a great example of a startup that applies a high level of discipline to assessing and testing its medium risk capacity. They defined what's safe to experiment with, what might impact customers, and what's reversible. They embraced a degree of internal clumsiness during testing phases and reserved perfection for core service delivery. Medium capacity is not a green light. It's a yellow light. Move forward, but with awareness and caution.

5. **Always consider the risk of doing nothing.** As Rob Barnes put it during our interview, "I wish more people asked: *What will happen if we don't do this?*" That question flips the innovation conversation from fear-based paralysis to purpose-drive action. Avoiding risk can feel safer, but the cost of inaction often compounds into declining engagement, shrinking market share, and waning relevance. These are not overnight occurrences; they're slow leaks. But by the time those cracks get exposed, they're often harder and more expensive to fix.

Regardless of your organization's risk capacity level, both data and discipline are needed. The sweet spot for innovation occurs where leaders align their data strategy with an accurate read on their organization's risk capacity—and then identify data-influenced boundaries that reflect that reality. It's not a one-time decision; it's an ongoing leadership practice. Like muscles, your capacity for risk can be stretched and strengthened over time. With each well-designed experiment, when boundaries are clear, your organization can become more resilient, more agile, and more capable of making bold moves, without wandering blindly.

YOUR TURN TO THINK DIFFERENTLY

When you understand your risk capacity and establish boundaries, you earn the right to experiment. You create a culture where trying—and even failing—are not signs of recklessness, but rather of resilience. That's when you shift the narrative from "We can't afford to fail" to "We can't afford to wait."

1. What's one experiment your organization could run with
    minimal downside but potentially high learning value?

2. How might your team's approach to innovation change if
    you measured attempts alongside outcomes?

3. What's the real risk of maintaining the status quo in your
    industry or field?

CHAPTER 3

The Boundaries We Move

Rules aren't always made to be broken—but some certainly are. Namely, I'm speaking about those unexamined processes and policies that companies and associations keep around simply because "we've always done it this way."

This innovation-killer of a refrain often signals not a fixed rule, but an opportunity in disguise. During my time as director of membership and marketing at the Association Forum, I inherited a traditional approach to marketing our annual conference. For over a decade, the organization had relied on a familiar formula: buy lists, design print pieces, and mail them. And it worked . . . until it didn't. Response rates started to dip, but the process carried on unchanged.

When I joined the staff, certain elements of my work—budget, timing, and target audience—were all locked in. But I wanted to use some of my budget to experiment with a different, more creative approach. I pitched a few alternatives, but my boss wasn't interested.

"We've always mailed brochures," he said. The implication was clear: Don't mess with what's known, even if it's not working so well anymore. Leadership perceived the risk of changing "what we've always done" as too high to even consider.

This changed when the organization hired a new CEO in late 2003. Gary LaBranche, who went on to become CEO of RIMS, the Risk Management Society, brought with him a different mindset—one rooted in experimentation and trust. He understood how to evaluate risk and explored the potential consequences of changing nothing. Knowing I would likely have his support, I started proposing new ways to market and sell membership and conference registrations.

In 2006, I proposed diverting part of the original budget to a then-untested medium to market an event: YouTube. I wanted to create a video that could be shared with our members and past attendees. Something funny and interesting that they could, in turn, share with their networks. LaBranche was willing to test an assumption that direct mail may not be the most effective way to attract new attendees to our conference. He created a safe space for me to experiment by giving me the freedom to create something new. LaBranche didn't ask me to blow up the budget or timeline; he simply gave me permission to experiment and even made it okay if we failed—as long as we learned something from the effort.

So, we created *Association Professionals Throughout History*.[1] We wrote the script and storyboards internally and hired an animator to bring it to life. The video was sent to members and past attendees with a link to register at the end.

The result? We boosted attendance by 20 percent, and, more importantly, first-time attendance rose by more than 30 percent. People who had previously overlooked our printed brochures now stopped, clicked, and laughed—then registered for our event. That's the power of moving one boundary while honoring another. We didn't need to blow it all up; we just needed to challenge the right constraint.

Boundaries exist for a reason. They keep things on track, on budget, and on time. But over time, those same boundaries can become invisible barriers, quietly stalling innovation and progress.

While boundaries help teams understand the limits—how far they can go, how much they can spend, how fast they can move—it's essential to regularly re-evaluate those boundaries to avoid getting trapped in outdated assumptions.

Too often, I've seen organizations try to innovate inside of constraints that no longer serve them. They follow rules set years ago, never questioning whether those rules are still relevant or necessary. In other words, while thinking *inside* the box can unlock hidden power, it really all depends on the box. As leaders, it's our job to make sure the reasons behind your boundaries are still relevant, valid, and valuable. Some walls you find yourself in will prove to be essential constraints. Others have long outlived their purpose and may need to be moved back or even torn down altogether.

Take membership models, for example. After years of decline, driven by retirements and waning interest from younger professionals, many associations have started rethinking how they define access and value. Traditionally, associations offered a mix of free and paid benefits, with membership acting as the gatekeeper to premium offerings. Over time, governments began requiring that association journals and publications be made publicly accessible.[2] Many other core services, like advocacy, industry guidelines, and timely updates, are already available to members and nonmembers alike.

This shift makes it even harder to promote, or even sometimes defend, membership dues.

Organizations may understand the need to change. They explore new options like tiered pricing (e.g., "good, better, best") to attract and retain members. But then fear creeps in. *What if current members all downgrade to the lowest tier?* To counter this, some assign the most-used benefits to the middle tier, aligning member values with the bulk of the existing structure.

Still, tough questions remain. If the most valuable benefits, such as advocacy, publications, and guidelines, are free, will things like networking, volunteer leadership, or a discount on continuing education be enough to justify the cost of membership dues? For many organizations, after a long and thorough review, the answer is *maybe not*. And so, they retreat, defaulting to the familiar one-size-fits-all membership model they know, even when the need for change is clear.

But this is exactly the moment to move the boundary. To ask, *What if the constraints we're working within aren't fixed, but flexible? What if reimagining the parameters is the very spark we need to unlock growth?*

When organizations cling to outdated boundaries, even the best intentions can fall flat. But when they question those boundaries— when they ask not just, *What should we do differently?* but also, *What unexamined assumptions are we still working within?*—that's when they begin to unlock new possibilities.

That's exactly what happened outside the world of associations, in an entirely different setting: a public library and a national crisis around access to books.

The Brooklyn Public Library Reimagines Boundaries

In 2022, book bans were sweeping across the United States. Titles disappeared from school shelves, and debates erupted in school board meetings. While much of the country's libraries and schools reacted defensively, the Brooklyn Public Library asked a different question: *What if the real issue wasn't the bans themselves, but the outdated policies that made it so easy to block access in the first place?*[3]

Amy Mikel, director of customer experience at the Brooklyn Public Library, found herself returning to that question over and over again. Like most public libraries, if you lived in Brooklyn, or had proof that you did, you could apply for a library card and to check out physical and digital materials. If you didn't? You didn't have access to their vast collection of books.

In the age of digital books, Amy and her team began to wonder, *Why does geography still define the boundary of who we serve?* The infrastructure already existed to deliver eBooks and audiobooks digitally. So why cling to old policies or constraints? Why couldn't the Brooklyn Public Library open up their catalog to the thousands of teenagers across the country who didn't have a library card?

That's how the *Books Unbanned* initiative was born. The library began offering free digital library cards to teens across the country, regardless of where they lived. Through this program, they redrew the boundary lines of public service. Instead of a borough, they now served a nation.

They didn't abandon structure entirely. In fact, they preserved many critical parameters—privacy safeguards, age-appropriate access, and usage limits—to ensure the system remained manageable and secure. By reevaluating which policies were truly necessary, they were able to move outdated boundaries and make space for something new.

It wasn't long before thousands of teens across the US began signing up. They sent emails and social media messages filled with gratitude and stories. Some lived in towns where banned book lists had grown so long that entire shelves of their libraries sat empty. Others faced rigid ID policies that made it nearly impossible to obtain a library card. Some teens didn't feel safe asking permission from a parent or teacher. For many, *Books Unbanned* wasn't just about reading; it was about privacy, autonomy, and the fundamental right to read and learn.

Amy and her colleagues read every email and every social media post their new group of patrons sent them. They recognized that what seemed like a small act, issuing a library card, was actually profound. It represented access, freedom, and trust.

What the Brooklyn Public Library did so effectively was to identify the hidden parameters that had long shaped their service delivery—parameters that were more habitual than strategic. Geography had once been a practical constraint. Now it was just a vestigial boundary, rendered obsolete by new tech. By surfacing this invisible parameter and questioning its continued relevance, they were able to refine their mission and dramatically expand their reach.

This is also where I came in. Amy reached out to my company, Avenue M Group, for help. She wanted to understand the broader landscape: *How many libraries had policies that created or maintained unintentional barriers to access? Were there systemic patterns? Could policy changes make a meaningful difference?* In other words, she needed to define the essential constraints and move the ones that were out of date.

The project was led by my colleague, Emily Thomas, a senior researcher who spearheaded a study of nearly 1,500 libraries across the country. She and our Avenue M team conducted interviews, focus groups, and surveys with librarians across the country. They dove into the fine print of library card policies, including identification requirements, residency proof, age restrictions, and parental permissions.

Some libraries hadn't updated their policies in over a decade. Others required multiple forms of ID, residency documentation, or parental consent—all barriers that disproportionately impacted teens, especially those who were housing-insecure, undocumented, or in vulnerable family situations. By examining the constraints or boundaries, our team discovered access to information wasn't just a matter of supply. It was also a matter of policy.

This story illustrates a central theme of this chapter: Boundaries don't just confine; they define. Once you've mapped where they lie, you can identify which ones still serve a purpose, which don't, and which can be moved. The Brooklyn Public Library didn't try to eliminate all boundaries. What they did instead was far more powerful: They mapped them.

They examined which boundaries were necessary (like safeguarding privacy or managing budgets) versus those that had outlived their purpose. Once they had that clarity, they got to work recommending changes to the policies that no longer made sense.

This is a core idea of this book: that true innovation isn't always about "coloring outside of the lines"—essentially painting all over the walls. It's about understanding the real dimensions of your particular canvases and knowing how to expand or redraw the lines of your painting within those. Boundaries don't always have to be limits. Sometimes they can be moved.

In the case of Brooklyn Public Library, moving the boundaries led to a long-needed change. Using the research Emily and our team conducted, the Brooklyn Public Library sparked deeper conversations, not only inside their own organization but also across library systems nationwide. They now collaborate with other libraries to revisit and reimagine their own access policies.

One of the most powerful lessons from this partnership is that constraints aren't always the enemy. Sometimes, they point the way forward or point out what needs to be moved or changed. When an organization takes the time to examine where its boundaries lie and why they exist, it gains the power to decide what to protect and what to change.

The *Books Unbanned* story also reminded me that the most effective change doesn't always come from tearing down walls. Sometimes it comes from knowing exactly where the walls currently stand, who put them there, what purpose they serve, and whether or not they're essential, "weight-bearing" boundaries. That clarity turns fixed limitations into dynamic, movable ones.

Structured Creativity Spurs Innovation

While the Brooklyn Public Library redrew policy boundaries to expand access, software engineer Sam Ritchie saw innovation emerge by defining the ones that would help guide more creative thinking among a team of software engineers.

Throughout Ritchie's career, he's created systems and developed models at some of the most well-known innovation labs and organizations in the world—TED Conferences, the Moonshot Factory, X (formerly known as Twitter), Stripe, and now his own Boulder-based startup FrogRocket Labs[4]—but he doesn't talk about innovation in terms of "limitless creativity." Instead, he talks about structure, modular systems, and designing within mathematical rules. For Ritchie, innovation happens when you stop aimlessly wandering and start building within a well-designed box.

However, long before Ritchie built streaming data platforms at Twitter or designed modular robot minds at FrogRocket Labs, he quietly absorbed a very different kind of lesson about creativity from his own parents. Bill Ritchie and Andrea Barthello founded ThinkFun (originally Binary Arts) in the basement of their Virginia home in 1985. Their mission: "To translate the brilliant ideas of the craziest mathematicians, engineers and inventors into simple toys that can be appreciated by boys and girls around the world."

As a kid, Sam was surrounded by puzzles, games, and toy prototypes, but what resonated with him wasn't just the playfulness; it was the structure. He remembers preferring Lego kits with clear instructions over freeform builds, and he often worried that following the rules too closely made him "not creative." Ironically, that early relationship with constraints, the kind his parents had transformed into a business, would become a core feature of his work.

This formative philosophy from childhood drove one of Ritchie's earlier projects at Twitter. At the time, according to Ritchie, Twitter processed more than twenty thousand user tweets a second, and the product teams struggled to generate useful analytics that were efficient enough to give real-time feedback without taking days or weeks to process such high volumes of data. Faced with this challenge, Ritchie and his team built a system that only allowed specific types of data transformations, ones that obeyed a core mathematical property.

"You could only use data structures that played by one rule of math," he explained. "But once teams accepted that constraint, they started thinking totally differently. They began searching for all these weird data structures—ones they'd never used before—that happened to fit the rule. And those structures unlocked new product ideas."

So, what was this rule? It was a basic principle: Whatever data you combined had to be combined in a consistent, predictable way. That meant you could group lots of data together—like chunks of past activity—and then easily add in real-time updates without redoing everything. If your data also didn't care about the order things were added, you could make the process even faster and more efficient.

By designing around this one rule, the team unlocked a whole new way of building software. "They even created a toolset that ended up being used at massive scale—like in Apple's iMessage system, where it quietly powered millions of messages behind the scenes," Ritchie shared.

In other words, the limitation sparked a new kind of creativity. "The constraint," Ritchie said, "became the feature."

Instead of asking, *What do we want to build?* they flipped the model to *What's possible within these rules?* That shift, from open-ended brainstorming to constraint-driven creativity, unlocked a host of new tools.

Similarly, when creative teams face unlimited possibilities, they often struggle to pick a direction and get started. By establishing clearer, more focused parameters, leaders reduce this heavy thinking and activate the brain's problem-solving capabilities instead. The constraints enable and empower rather than limit.

We often assume that innovation means breaking down all barriers. Ritchie, however, unlocked much more creative potential by examining and carefully choosing which boundaries to keep, which to scrap, and importantly, which just needed to move.

That distinction underpins a wide range of innovations throughout Ritchie's career, including his early developer tools. In 2011, engineers were forced to reduce rich, complex data to numbers and strings just to move it across a wire. Nobody questioned it. They simply accepted the friction as normal. "People had amnesia," Ritchie said. "They forgot that in every other part of their work, that kind of loss would be unacceptable."

So, he built a fix—and it unlocked a wave of ideas. At the time, the system could only handle basic data types, like strings and numbers. But in real-world programming, people use more complex structures—lists, sets, or dictionaries—to make sense of information. Without a way to carry those structures through the system, users had to break everything down into basic parts, run their data jobs, and then reassemble the pieces after. Being so clunky and inefficient, this system severely limited their programming possibilities.

Sam's fix was to integrate a smarter data-handling tool that automatically recognized and supported these complex structures across different machines. Suddenly, people didn't have to do all that manual prep work. They could think bigger, experiment faster, and see their ideas more clearly. "Suddenly, people could think about more complex models," he explained. "They could visualize what they were doing. Everything got more generative."

Ritchie believes this happens all the time, both in software and in human organizations. We work within invisible constraints, unaware of how much they shape our thinking. We don't rebel against, or even question, these arbitrary limits. Sometimes, we're so used to the walls that we don't even see them anymore. We simply stop having ideas that our current understanding of the system can't support.

That's why Ritchie emphasizes the importance of both good tools and good boundaries. They don't just help us get things done; they also show us where opportunities lie. "Innovation dies when people resign themselves to pain," he told me.

This mindset isn't just for engineers. It applies just as much to leaders, teams, and organizations. Too many of us spend our days inside systems that nudge us toward the same, safe decisions over and over again. We avoid change not because we're incapable, but because the current, long-standing conditions don't make new ideas easy.

"People don't need to be told what to think," Ritchie said. "They need tools—and parameters—that make better thinking easier."

Take Apple, for example. Steve Jobs believed that technology should be accessible to everyone. To achieve this, Jobs and Jony Ive, Apple's chief design officer, focused on reducing complexity, based on the belief that great design should be invisible. As a result, the iPhone's pinch-to-zoom gesture was so intuitive that users immediately figured it out, without tutorials.[5]

One common parameter embraced by Apple is a version of the "five-minute rule"—a productivity hack aimed at overcoming procrastination by committing to a task for just five minutes. Apple reframed this idea for their purposes: If a product or feature takes more than five minutes for a user to understand or gain value from, it's likely too complex. This principle guides Apple's rapid prototyping and user-first design strategy. The goal is to distill a product to its most essential features—those that delight users or help them become productive almost immediately. By minimizing friction and focusing on intuitive interactions, Apple ensures its technology conforms to human behavior, not the other way around.[6]

For your own organization, this might mean establishing parameters like "solutions must reduce customer service calls by 20 percent" or "new features must enable instant support" rather than vague mandates like "improve customer experience." The specific parameters will vary based on your industry and strategic priorities, but the principle remains the same: transforming data into clear boundaries that guide innovation, without prescribing exactly how to innovate.

How to Develop Effective Creative Parameters

To create effective parameters that genuinely enable rather than restrict, consider these guidelines:

1. **Focus on outcomes, not methods.** Too often, teams get handed a solution disguised as a goal. When leaders say, "Build a patient-focused app," they may unintentionally box creativity. By skipping the *what* and jumping straight to the *how*, they limit innovation before it begins.

   Instead, define the outcome you wish to achieve and let the team explore how to get there. A better parameter might state a specific goal: say, reducing patient wait time by 30 percent over the next twelve months. One team might redesign the scheduling interface; another might deploy SMS check-in reminders; a third might shift some consultations to asynchronous video updates. Each of these solutions could be right, but not one will surface if you only ask for a better app. Don't micromanage creativity; instead, create a clear boundary (goal) while leaving room for multiple solution approaches.

2. **Make parameters measurable.** Vague parameters can create more confusion than clarity. Parameters like "improve the patient experience" may sound strategic, but they're hard to act on. Why? Because they're also hard to measure.

   Instead, replace the word "improve" with more specific, actionable metrics. For example, "increase weekly active users by 15 percent" both clarifies the goal and focuses potential solutions. Similarly, "achieve a net promoter score of fifty or higher" helps teams focus on creating specific audiences and experiences that, if enhanced, would result in more referrals. Ensure your parameters include specific metrics that teams can track to know if they're succeeding.

3. **Limit parameters to three to five per initiative.** In chapter 1, I shared the phrase, "You can do anything but not everything." In other words, when everything is a priority, nothing is. Too many parameters can overwhelm a team. Identify the three to five most critical boundaries that matter for success, according to your top goals.

  If you are having trouble prioritizing, conduct a quick survey of your team and ask them to identify the top five most critical ones. Then ask them to select the single most critical goal among these. A survey provides the opportunity to gather quick feedback without the groupthink or unconscious biases that naturally occur during a team meeting. This constraint isn't just about focus; it's about capacity. For example, if your organization wants to redesign its annual conference, and an initial brainstorming session yielded a list of seventeen parameters, narrow them down to three:

  1. *Increase the first-time attendee return rate by 25 percent.*
  2. *Improve speaker ratings to 4.5 or higher.*
  3. *Add two new networking formats for introverts.*

  This will give teams clarity and permission to ignore everything not primarily focused on achieving these three outcomes.

4. **Know when to move a parameter.** While well-designed parameters give teams the structure they need to be more creative, rigid ones no longer serve the mission and can stall progress. The goal isn't to set parameters in stone; it's to set them intentionally, revisit them regularly, and move them when new data, insights, or circumstances demand change.

   Ask yourself:

   - *Has the original assumption behind this parameter changed?*
   - *Are teams running into the same challenges and not finding creative solutions?*
   - *Has the environment (technology, policy, audience) shifted?*
   - *Is the current boundary serving strategic goals simply preserving old habits?*

   The key is not to abandon parameters at the first sign of resistance, but to treat them as living tools. If a team falls short of a metric despite their creativity and energy, it might not be a performance issue. It could be a sign that the parameter needs to shift.

   When the Brooklyn Public Library wanted to expand access to its collection of digital books, it uncovered a legacy constraint that could be moved—requiring someone to live within the geographic boundaries set back when libraries were limited to physically distributing material collections. It started when Amy Mikel and her colleagues asked important questions: *Does this parameter still serve its purpose? Does it prevent access in a digital world where location no longer needs to be a barrier?*

   By re-examining that constraint, the Brooklyn Public Library didn't eliminate a structure; they simply moved the line to better serve their mission: access to knowledge, especially for those facing real barriers.

5. **Test parameters with teams.** Even the best-designed parameters can fall apart once they've been set. Before finalizing parameters, test them with implementation teams. *Do they provide sufficient clarity to start working on solutions? Do they leave room for creative approaches?* If not, ask for feedback and refine them. A quick pilot, or even a testing working session, can expose hidden flaws or friction points.

   Teams may find that one metric contradicts another or that meeting one parameter undermines another department's goals. By testing parameters before committing time and money to them, you can better ensure that they will lead to your desired outcomes. For example, a logistics company may set a parameter to "deliver 95 percent of orders within forty-eight hours." While this sounds good, to accomplish it, one department may need to skip quality checks. Instead, a new parameter to "maintain customer complaints to below 1 percent" might be more realistic. The combination of speed and satisfaction could create a better boundary for innovation.

6. **Connect to a broader purpose.** Effective parameters aren't arbitrary—they connect directly to organizational mission and strategy. Without purpose, parameters can feel bureaucratic. Communicate the connection to the organization's mission, values, or strategy to increase buy-in. For example, instead of "decrease member churn," an association could set a parameter to "reduce member churn by 15 percent, because every retained member strengthens our advocacy efforts and builds community."

   Context matters. Share the *why* in internal documents, presentations, and kickoff meetings. Show how each parameter connects to something bigger than the metric itself.

When parameters are designed thoughtfully, they don't just manage risk or enforce structure. They spark creativity, focus effort, and reveal what really matters. Whether you're building a robot, launching a product, or designing a member experience, the boundaries you set aren't just protective—they're directional. They show your team *where* to play, *why* to care, and *how* to win.

But clarity isn't just a top-down exercise. Often, the most valuable insights about boundaries don't come from leadership; they come from the people closest to the customer, member, or the delivery of the product or service.

I've heard this from interns and entry-level professionals who struggle with outdated onboarding processes, and from frontline staffers who spend hours managing some outdated tool maintained out of pure, unexamined inertia. I have also seen this come up in association representatives who ask for feedback from former members who let their memberships lapse—but don't use this information to make any meaningful changes.

Too often, frontline voices are missing from the conversation. In many organizations, silos and silence are the real innovation killers. It's not that teams don't have ideas; it's that many times, no one is listening.

That's why Part Two focuses on how to build a culture where every voice can challenge assumptions, identify the friction points that may be overlooked, and help leaders see where boundaries need to be set or be shifted.

YOUR TURN TO THINK DIFFERENTLY

1. Which policies in your organization exist simply because "we've always done it that way" and should be re-examined?
2. What could be possible if you questioned one major assumption about how your work must be done?
3. What are the essential constraints, and what are some outdated limitations within your organization?

Part Two

Voice

CHAPTER 4

Culture of Curiosity

In my mid-twenties, I landed a job as a marketing and public relations specialist at the Culinary School of Kendall College. I was the youngest person on staff by more than a decade, and as a trained photojournalist, I had no direct marketing experience. But while I didn't come with a long résumé in higher ed recruitment, I did bring something else: I understood the mindset of our prospective students—many of whom were, like me, making a major career change in their twenties or later and wondering if it was too late to change lanes and start fresh.

Over the years, Kendall College has produced some of the world's leading chefs, including notable alumni like Beverly Kim and Jose Garces, who both won the prestigious James Beard Award, considered the pinnacle of US culinary accolades. My role? To develop the student recruitment materials and attract media attention. As a department of one, I reported directly to the dean of admissions.

What made this job stand out wasn't just the spectacular cafeteria food made by professional chefs-in-training, but also the leadership team. Most of the executives had been there for twenty years or more. Despite my youth and limited experience, they did something that left a lasting impact on me—they listened. They asked for my input, encouraged my ideas, and created an environment where I felt safe speaking up, even when I wasn't sure if my ideas would work.

Not every idea was a home run; in fact, some fell far short of our goals. Still, the leadership team encouraged both active brainstorming and ongoing experimentation with new ideas—even when some flopped. Looking back, I now see that all creative iteration took place within the context of clearly defined goals and parameters.

One clear boundary we repeatedly faced as we tried to compete against much larger schools was our very small recruitment budget. Having limited funds meant I needed to get creative and use freelancers rather than hiring an experienced marketing agency. Some of the ideas we came up with were fresh; others failed miserably. Through it all, I always understood the limits. I also knew that, within those parameters, I had the freedom and support—indeed, the directive—to try new ideas. Even if they failed.

Having just gone through the college selection process myself, I vividly recalled my mailbox overflowing with brochures that all looked the same. It felt like every school had dipped into the same pool of stock photos or recreated the same scene: a group of students sitting cross-legged under a tree, smiling intently at a professor. I knew from experience this almost never happened. And yet, there it was, again and again, including on the brochure for Kendall College.

I had an idea: What if we scrapped the posed perfection and showed the real, messy, lived-in version of campus life? I proposed hiring a freelance photographer to capture candid images of actual students, in real moments—not models, not staged.

When I shared the idea during a staff meeting, the initial reaction was silence. Then, to my surprise, my boss said, "Yes, but just for one recruitment campaign." I pushed back, explaining that one try wouldn't be enough to learn anything meaningful. He agreed to a longer test as long as I stuck to the budget and timeline.

The result? We nearly doubled the number of prospective students requesting information about the college. That campaign marked a turning point for me. I was new to marketing, having just transitioned from photojournalism, and I wasn't sure if this new role would give me space to be creative or even have a voice. This project reminded me of what I loved about journalism: seeing a story unfold, capturing something honest, and sharing it in a way that moved people. It gave me that same spark, that same sense of purpose.

That experience shaped how I think about leadership and innovation to this day. It taught me that age, title, or tenure shouldn't dictate who gets to have a voice. Sometimes the freshest ideas come from the person with the least experience—but with the most relevant and valuable perspective.

This idea that "every voice matters" may sound simple. It's also a claim that most leadership teams love to make—but very, very few of them actually practice what they preach. Those companies that actually follow through on this promise tend to stand out and scale up, sometimes dramatically.

Case in point? Terence Reilly. Reilly is the master marketer behind both the rebirth of Crocs and the Stanley Quencher. When I learned that one person led both brand reinvention campaigns—and that he credits both successes to his open-door policy for ensuring good ideas can bubble up from anywhere within the organization—I had to learn more.

Crocs: From Punchlines to Profits

When Reilly was the chief marketing officer at Crocs, a young woman named Toria Roth knocked on his door and asked if he could give her a minute. Roth had just moved into her first full-time role at Crocs after finishing an internship with the company. Reilly welcomed her into his office, where she showed him a photo of the rising rapper Post Malone wearing a pair of Crocs.

As Reilly later shared in a *Harvard Business Review* podcast,[1] "He wasn't wearing them with any sort of irony; he just was wearing them. And [Roth] said, 'This could be something for Crocs.' So, I reached out to the folks that manage Post Malone, and I said, 'Hey, would you be interested in a partnership or a collaboration where Post could create his own Crocs?'"

That knock on Reilly's door led to the company's first celebrity collaboration. Its popularity exceeded all expectations, even crashing the Crocs' website when it went live. At the time, as Reilly pointed out in the *Harvard Business Review* interview, "Crocs was a meme." And not exactly the good kind.

"The meme was [joking that] 'those holes are where your dignity leaks out.' We knew, and certainly I knew, that we had a classic; we just needed to create more relevance for the brand. We didn't have an awareness problem at Crocs; we had a relevance opportunity. Post Malone was that real quick injection of relevance, and once he was on board, it allowed me to call almost any artist or any brand to collaborate."[2, 3]

Reilly ties the successful turnaround at Crocs to both this open-door policy that welcomes all voices and to the company's comfort with taking a risk. Don't forget that this was in the early 2000s, before Post Malone became the household name he is today. Plus, his face was already covered in tattoos, a far cry from the typical profile of an early Crocs owner (namely, boaters, due to their overall waterproofing and slip-proof, non-marking soles). Post Malone may not have reflected their target demographic—he certainly wasn't a middle-aged boater or gardener who preferred comfort over style. But he had a loyal fan base. And he truly loved wearing Crocs.

"When you have that authenticity, you have gold," Reilly added. "That you can't really manufacture, as hard as you try. And we had something that was risky at the time; walking into senior leadership at Crocs to tell them we should be betting on Post Malone was a bit of a career risk for me, I'm sure. Taking that risk and listening was the key. Listening to that young associate who had her finger on the pulse of culture, listening to the consumer, and having the courage to act on it."

When Reilly became the CEO at Stanley, he brought the same mindset: listen to those who are closest to the customer, and don't be afraid to take calculated, informed risks. But Reilly's approach went beyond intuition; at Crocs (and later at Stanley) he implemented a structured strategy to assess and act on opportunities.

Several Layers of Risk Assessment

1. **Vetting insights across levels.** Reilly actively pursued and encouraged input from various organizational levels, ensuring ideas were not just top-down but also grassroots.
2. **Triangulating strategy with constraints.** Before scaling, Reilly considered manufacturing capabilities, supply chain logistics, and brand identity. He wanted to ensure that any expansion or shift wouldn't compromise the company's core values or efficiency.
3. **Leveraging defined boundaries for creativity.** By focusing on a specific audience, Reilly could gather data and customize his marketing and product development efforts to their needs, minimizing the risk of trying to be everything to everyone.

The Quencher: Embracing Influencer Culture

When Reilly got to Stanley, the first thing he did was to implement these same leadership techniques he developed at Crocs. Almost immediately after becoming the CEO of Stanley, Reilly began to interview his colleagues and find out what was working and what wasn't working. That's when Lauren Solomon, a sales associate, told Reilly about a group of women in Utah who absolutely loved the Stanley forty-ounce Quencher.

In the early 2010s, you were far more likely to see a Stanley thermos tucked in a camping backpack or your grandfather's garage than in some trendy influencer's social posts. The century-old brand was mostly known for its reliable and rugged hammertone green. Their products, though durable, had not kept up to date with the water bottle trend then rapidly growing in the US.

The turning point came in 2019 when Ashlee LeSueur, co-founder of *The Buy Guide* (*TBG*), a lifestyle blog and Instagram account, discovered the forty-ounce Stanley Quencher at a Bed Bath & Beyond store. Impressed by its functionality and design, she started giving it to friends and featured it on *TBG*'s platform. The response was overwhelming; every time they linked the product, it sold out almost instantly.

Then, soon after *TBG* featured the Quencher, Stanley discontinued the product, due to overall lackluster sales. LeSueur, a true Quencher believer, didn't want to give up that easily. Determined to keep the product alive, *TBG* reached out to Stanley, but initially they received little response. At the time, *TBG* had a small following on Instagram, and Stanley didn't have much social media presence . . . until that young Stanley sales associate, Lauren Solomon, knocked on the door of Reilly's office.

Solomon had seen a Stanley Quencher featured on a social media post from Emily Maynard, then a contestant on the television show, *The Bachelor*. After Maynard took to Instagram to show off her *TBG*-gifted Stanley Quencher, Solomon knew it was time to approach their new CEO, Reilly.

Once again, Reilly opened his door. Once again, a young woman brought him a social media post that seemed worlds away from his company's target audience. And, once again, *he listened*. He realized that this could turn into Stanley's "Post Malone" moment—just the demographic crossover opportunity they needed to become more relevant.

Stanley proposed a wholesale arrangement that required *The Buy Guide* to purchase ten thousand units up front. Taking a significant financial risk of their own, they ordered five thousand units, which sold out in five days. A subsequent order of another five thousand units sold out in just an hour.[4] This caught Reilly's attention. He knew from his experience with Crocs that this could ignite the change Stanley needed to level up.

Recognizing the untapped potential, Reilly shifted the company's marketing strategy to focus on a broader demographic, particularly women aged twenty-five to fifty—a group that *TBG* had effectively engaged.[5]

Under Reilly's leadership, Stanley embraced influencer marketing and expanded its product line with new colors and designs, transforming the Quencher from a niche item into a mainstream cultural phenomenon. By 2023, Stanley's annual revenue soared from $73 million in 2019 to approximately $750 million, largely due to the Quencher's popularity.

When we talk about creating space for innovation, we often think of freedom. We think of open doors, open minds, and open brainstorming sessions with colleagues. But innovation thrives when there are boundaries or constraints. Not just when other voices can be heard, but also when leaders actively create a safe space to experiment and take risks. This approach nurtures a culture of bounded psychological safety, a high-support, high-challenge environment where everyone can contribute and innovate among essential parameters and clear priorities.

When Reilly joined Crocs, he had to work with a brand that was viewed as functional. Rather than fighting this constraint, Reilly leaned into its quirky identity and reframed it as a strength. He embraced the "ugly but comfortable" perception. Crocs also had a loyal following of nurses, gardeners, chefs, and kids. He amplified the loyal segments first, never forgetting they were the core customers.

When Reilly pursued the collaboration with Post Malone, it was a risk. But he didn't bet the entire company on this risk. He made a minimal upfront investment to test the waters. When he listened to his team, it did it with intention, by asking specific questions about what worked and what didn't. These constraints ensured Reilly could explore new ideas, or innovate, while minimizing financial risks to the company. He embraced boundaries instead of eliminating them. Reilly focused narrowly, tested ideas within constraints, and scaled after validating them.

At Crocs, the boundaries were clear. Their limits included budget constraints and a successful, if demographically limited, brand perception. Their challenge? Broader cultural relevance. So, when his youngest and newest team members brought him ideas, Reilly didn't dismiss them. He leaned in. He listened. He understood the risks and still took the shots. Those two single decisions reframed these brands' relevance and sent the revenue of two nationally acclaimed brands soaring, opening doors to future collaborations. It also sent a key message to his entire staff: *Your voice matters.*

Targeted Input and Calculated Risks

Reilly didn't just walk into Crocs or Stanley and blow up their systems. He asked questions. He listened. He operated within the clear, coherent boundaries of the brand's legacy, heritage, durability, function, and operating budgets. Finally, using vital input from junior staff, he found new openings.

That initial insight from a Crocs sales associate became the spark. The partnership with *TBG* was a risk. But it was a calculated one made possible because Reilly trusted the people closest to the customer, and he believed that big leaps often start small.

Boundaries didn't limit innovation at either of Reilly's companies. They instead defined the playground. They made it safe to take bold shots without risking everything, and they tapped the voices of those closest to the consumers.

I like to compare this approach with companies that attempt to "boil the sea" by pursuing broad, undefined markets without a clear strategy. In trying to be everything to everyone, most companies fail—both to implement the right strategic ideas for leveling up and to generate such ideas from their teams in the first place. It's always a challenge pulling fresh, new insights from a team that feels direction-less, confused, and overwhelmed by all the possibilities.

One well-documented example of a company that took this flawed approach is JCPenney. When Ron Johnson, formerly of Apple, joined JCPenney, he wanted to transform the company from an aging department store to a hip, modern retailer. He eliminated coupons and sales, revamped store layouts, and tried to attract a more upscale, trend-driven audience. However, this approach failed because Johnson ignored their price-sensitive core customer base. The new strategy was both too generic and too upscale, alienating existing shoppers without clearly attracting a new group. The company didn't target a specific demographic or customer segment. Instead, it tried to appeal to "everyone" with broad, undifferentiated strategies. Rather than piloting smaller changes and learning from the results, Johnson rolled out massive overhauls nationwide. As a result, sales plummeted with losses soaring to nearly $1 billion in one year, and Johnson was fired after seventeen months. The company spent years trying to undo the damage.[6]

At Kendall College, the leadership didn't just say they had an open-door policy and embraced trying new things; they also created conditions for someone like me—with little to no experience but a fresh perspective—to contribute.

I didn't realize it then, but I was experiencing what psychologists call high-support, high-challenge leadership: You feel trusted and empowered, but never alone or directionless. That combination defines bounded psychological safety, and it changed how I think about risk.

Nearly a decade after I left Kendall College, I found myself in a leadership role with the chance to practice one of my core beliefs: that every voice should be heard. As chief marketing officer (CMO) at a membership organization, I inherited a long-standing practice for welcoming new members. Each one received an oversized pocket folder crammed with individual flyers outlining the many benefits of membership. Technically, we were providing everything someone needed to get involved. But practically? Engagement was low. And when it came time to renew, our first-year retention rate was extremely low.

Then one day, Diana Tapia, our membership coordinator, knocked on my office door and asked if she could try a different approach. Diana was the one stuffing the folders, mailing them out, and fielding frustrated calls from members who couldn't locate whatever specific details they needed among the mountain of onboarding documents. She knew we had a problem—and she had an idea.

Instead of the bulky folder that included everything we could think of, she proposed a sleek file folder branded with our organization's name and just a few essential materials inside. It was simple, clean, and—importantly—easy to store in a desk drawer. She also suggested spacing out the delivery of promotional items according to strategic timing and key priorities, rather than sending them all at once. It made sense. She understood our budget, and she understood our members.

That small change—born out of listening to someone who inter-acted with our members every day—led to a big result: First-year retention jumped, and engagement with our programs increased. All because one voice spoke up, and we listened.

Listening in the Quiet

When the global pandemic hit, like many other organizations, my company, Avenue M, had to shut down our physical office overnight and quickly figure out how to navigate a remote environment. The transition was abrupt, and no one knew when we'd return to the office. Our weekly staff meetings in our conference room shifted to the kitchen tables and laptop screens.

At first, we did what everyone did: we scrambled. There were tech issues, scheduling hiccups, and a sense of disconnect, not just from our clients but from each other. What surprised me most wasn't the logistics—it was how much I missed the casual, spontaneous moments: talking about our weekend plans, easy access to colleagues who could provide project or process insights, and the subtle sense of being part of something together.

The answer came from one of my team members, Emily Thomas, who was still early in her career and had been with my company for just a few years. She suggested we create weekly office hours where people could jump on a Zoom call—but the cameras stay off. It wouldn't be a Zoom happy hour or filled with team building activities or games. It wasn't forced fun. Her idea was simple: We would block off time on all of our calendars when we knew our colleagues would be free to connect.

We called it Virtual Office Hours. You could drop in to chat with colleagues, talk about your weekend plans, or ask for input or advice on a current project. When we hired Amanda, a recent graduate from Northwestern University, we were initially concerned about our fully remote workforce. We didn't have the welcome lunch or the opportunity for her to meet one-on-one, in person, with every member of the team. But we did have Virtual Office Hours. That's where she got a sense of the culture. Where she started to feel like she belonged.

What started as an experiment—an idea from someone who saw a gap—became part of the fabric of our company. Five years later, we still have Virtual Office Hours every Thursday. The same rules apply: no cameras, no pressure, no agenda. Just a space to be together.

Looking back, I see how powerful that small idea was. It wasn't just about remote work or pandemic adaptation. It was about creating a space that didn't demand productivity but allowed connection. It was about listening to someone who wasn't in a leadership role but saw something the rest of us had missed. Finally, it was about experimenting within constraints, trying something small and seeing if it stuck.

Emily's idea didn't require a budget or a new software platform. It didn't need a task force or approval from a board. It just needed one person to say, "What if . . . ?" and a leader willing to say, "Let's try."

In some ways, this small innovation mirrors the stories from Crocs and Stanley. In each case, success didn't come from trying to do everything or be everything. It came from noticing something specific. Creating a narrow lane. Testing something within a boundary. And building something meaningful from the inside out.

That's the beauty of ensuring other voices can be heard and working within boundaries. The playground fences and sandbox walls provide the structure needed to play and test new ideas. A place where ideas can take shape and grow. Because sometimes the most transformative changes come not from bold declarations or sweeping overhauls, but from a quiet Zoom call with no camera, no agenda, and a team willing to show up—just as they are.

It's often not the boldest idea that changes everything. Rather, it's the simple willingness to speak up and be heard. Just as importantly, it's the willingness of someone in a position of power to actually listen.

I didn't fully understand it at the time, but that moment from my early career, pitching a risky idea in a room full of seasoned professionals—that wasn't just about one campaign. It was about learning what kind of culture allows people to bring their best ideas forward.

Thinking back to my time at Kendall College, I believe that if my ideas had been dismissed or shut down, I probably would've looked for another place where I could contribute, be creative, and have a voice. Instead, I got lucky. I landed in an environment that valued ideas over titles and made space for experimentation. That changed everything—my confidence, my career, and eventually, the kind of leader I became.

You don't have to leave it up to luck. There are specific, actionable ways to create that kind of environment where experimentation is encouraged, boundaries are clear, and every voice is heard.

How to Create a Culture of Listening

1. **Conduct an annual "Closest to the Customer" listening tour.** Regardless of how long you've been with the organization, interview customer service reps, sales staff, interns, and entry-level professionals or admins. Ask, *What's working? What isn't working? What are customers asking for that we are not delivering? What opportunities might we be missing to expand our appeal beyond our current bounds?*

2. **Encourage small tests of new ideas with minimal downsides.** Make sure they can be scalable if they succeed. Identify which ideas might have the potential for high impact and high feasibility. When we tested the idea of Virtual Office Hours at my company, there was minimal downside to this experiment. Because my team already knew I embraced the idea of testing small ideas, a member of my team felt comfortable suggesting the idea.

3. **Get creative with high-impact ideas.** If something has the potential for high impact but low feasibility, don't immediately discount it. Instead, identify the boundaries and explore

the opportunities. In the case of Crocs partnership with Post Malone, Reilly believed it would have high impact because Malone had expressed his love for the shoes before being paid. He wasn't immediately certain of the feasibility, but he pursued the idea. The boundary he created was to ensure they didn't just approach some random celebrity who had a million followers on a social platform. By collaborating with someone who was already a genuine fan, Crocs created the partnership resonated with both existing customers and new audiences.

4. **Explore previously overlooked audience segments.** Stanley's iconic thermoses were long associated with a rugged, male demographic. But when a sales manager noticed the product gaining traction among women in Utah, Stanley tested a small batch sale with *TBG*. That under-tapped audience segment turned out to be transformational, fueling viral demand and increasing revenue nearly tenfold.

5. **Recognize and reward the messenger, not just the outcome.** Not every idea will work. Make sure your team knows your open-door policy is designed to encourage everyone on the team to share ideas. While the Virtual Office Hours was a success, we tried other ideas to create a sense of community that just didn't stick, such as the monthly "Lunch and Learns." Remote working had created the freedom to set different work hours and working in different time zones. After a few attempts, we decided to abandon the Lunch and Learn initiative. But while the idea flopped, I acknowledged the value of the idea itself. It also sparked a conversation about how best to collaborate and serve our clients within the freedom of setting our own working hours.

6. **Create a multi-vector open-door policy.** This can include (but shouldn't be limited to) simply knocking on your door. As more teams stay remote, consider how any team member may get access to your senior leadership team.

One way to accomplish this is to create a digital suggestion board visible to leadership and peers. Employees can upvote suggestions, add comments, or ask follow-up questions. Leadership should review the list weekly and keep everyone on the team updated on what is being considered and implemented.

Another way you can create an open-door policy is to create a program similar to what has been used at Netflix. It's called "Take the Hill." Rather than filtering ideas through layers of hierarchy, anyone within the organization can write a short proposal and take it straight to decision-makers. The goal is to create a direct line of access.

When, during my first marketing job, I pitched a bold idea in a room full of seasoned professionals, I didn't perceive it as some key formative moment. But it was. That single "yes" changed how I understood leadership, creativity, and risk. I was young and unproven—but someone listened.

That moment sparked a career-long belief that innovation isn't just reserved for the most experienced voice in the room. Whether it's a photojournalist-turned-marketer proposing real campus photos, a junior associate sharing a rapper's Instagram post, or a staff member suggesting camera-off Zoom calls, these moments are all rooted in the same truth: When everyone is trusted to try—and leaders are willing to listen—remarkable things happen.

YOUR TURN TO THINK DIFFERENTLY

1. Who in your organization might have valuable insights but rarely gets asked for their perspective?
2. What would change if you implemented a genuine "open-door policy" that reached beyond traditional hierarchy?
3. How could you create more opportunities for your newest team members to influence your most established practices?

CHAPTER 5

The Good Catch Model

Some of the most valuable lessons come from moments we wish we could do over.

Maybe your email campaign tried to be edgy, but instead it alienated a loyal customer base. Or maybe you used an AI tool to write and send an email—without fact-checking first—and it turned out to be full of errors.

In most organizations, leaders don't call much attention to such failures—and they certainly don't celebrate them as opportunities. We may praise people when they succeed, but we rarely reflect on or discuss their missteps. When someone does take a risk and fails, they're often left to carry that burden alone.

Imagine if you worked in a culture where the two examples I give not only get examined in a culture of safety but also celebrated. Where the edgy email that missed the mark sparks a conversation about brand voice and leads to new audience testing guidelines. Where the AI-generated message with factual errors becomes a case study that helps the team create an AI checklist to avoid future missteps.

What if, instead of hiding the error, your team unabashedly shared what happened, what they learned, and how they improved their process because of it? This is possible only in a culture rooted in bounded psychological safety, where the freedom to share mistakes exists within clearly defined expectations. Those moments of accountability, while uncomfortable, can strengthen your team's skills, build trust, and prevent bigger issues down the road. More importantly, they can create a culture where people feel safe to try. And when people feel safe to try, they're far more likely to experiment, innovate, and grow.

What if, as a leader, you could give people that "do-over" opportunity—to turn their loss into a new kind of win? Within that kind of culture, failure isn't the end of the story. It's the starting point for something better.

In my research for this book and discussions with friends and colleagues from a variety of industries, I've discovered there are different ways to create a culture that encourages experimentation, failure, speaking up, and learning from mistakes.

One of the most effective frameworks I've come across is the "Good Catch" model, originally used in healthcare to identify and share near-miss events before they escalate into real harm. Instead of punishing mistakes, this approach encourages employees to surface issues early—treating them as learning moments that benefit the entire organization.

The Best New Mistake Award

When Michael Alter was CEO of SurePayroll, he wanted to foster a culture that celebrated employees willing to experiment, even if they failed. Alter understood that to compete with larger, more established payroll companies like ADP—let alone capture a larger share of the market—he needed to diminish fear of failure within the organization. So, he created the "Best New Mistake Award."

Each year, during the company's "SureChoice Awards" ceremony, employees were encouraged to nominate themselves for the "Best New Mistake" award. Approximately forty nominees competed annually, highlighting the organization's commitment to transparency and continuous improvement. He awarded the top three entries gold, silver, and bronze awards, with the gold recipient receiving a $400 prize—double the amount awarded for other company awards.

This approach reframes mistakes as potential breakthroughs. They can even emerge as objective wins in the form of significant improvements and innovations. But their mistakes don't improve anything without constructive analysis. By formalizing the celebration of thoughtful mistakes, SurePayroll fostered a learning-driven culture anchored in bounded psychological safety—where employees were encouraged to take smart risks, knowing they'd be supported as long as they operated within clear business parameters.

The emphasis on "new" mistakes discourages repeated errors while promoting learning and growth through innovative thinking. In an *Inc.* magazine article from the July/August 2011 issue focused on "rethinking employee awards," Alter states, "Mistakes are the tuition you pay for success."

In her research on psychological safety, Harvard professor Amy Edmondson defines the term as "a belief that one will not be punished or humiliated for speaking up with ideas, questions, concerns, or mistakes."[1] In environments with strong bounded psychological safety, employees take more risks with how they work and communicate. They raise concerns early. They share insights freely. And they don't waste energy covering up honest mistakes.

Encourage Employees to Take More Shots

Years ago, Intuit—the company behind TurboTax, QuickBooks, and Mint—realized something important: If they wanted to become more innovative, they needed employees to take more chances. But there was one big question: *Would employees feel comfortable experimenting if they knew it could result in failure?*

Intuit's leadership team decided to implement some changes. Instead of focusing on "getting it right" and avoiding risk, they began celebrating both trial *and error*. Literally.

Similar to SurePayroll, Intuit created something their own "Failure Awards." At all-hands meetings, teams were invited onstage to talk about ideas they had tried that didn't work out. They established a set of criteria for experimenting and defined what "failure" meant.

The purpose of Intuit's Failure Awards was to praise intelligent failures: smart, well-designed experiments that just didn't go as expected—but potentially yielded some helpful insights. The process starts when an employee identifies a real customer problem. Next, a team will develop and test a hypothesis. When failure occurs, despite good planning and execution, the team captures the learnings to help inform future decisions.

The criteria, shared by Intuit, includes:[2]

1. Clear hypothesis
2. Rapid experimentation
3. Customer-centric focus
4. Measured outcomes
5. Actionable insights

One team, for example, built a new feature for small business owners. They followed all the right steps: user research, testing, a pilot rollout. But once it launched, it totally failed. Instead of sweeping it under the rug, they got up and shared what went wrong, what they learned, and what they'd do differently next time.

That moment, and the culture behind it, was inspired by Scott Cook, Intuit's co-founder. He had a great way of putting it: "We don't say, 'Take risks.' We say, 'Run lots of experiments.'"

That shift in language made a huge difference. Suddenly, people weren't afraid to try new things. They knew they'd be supported, even if something failed, as long as they grounded their experiment in sound, strategic methodology.[3] Because in the end, it wasn't about success or failure. It was about learning.

Intelligent Failure Versus Incompetence

Not all failures are created equal.

One of the most helpful distinctions in building a culture that embraces experimentation is the difference between a mistake that sparks growth and one that signals a problem. Psychological safety scholar Amy Edmondson defines the former as an "intelligent failure."[4]

An *intelligent failure* occurs in new territory, a domain of uncertain outcomes where assumptions get tested. These failures result from thoughtfully crafted and executed experiments. When you identify a real problem, design a smart test, and try something new, the results may not yield what you hoped, but you can still walk away with valuable insights that move your organization forward. This is the kind of failure you want.

On the other hand, *preventable failure* happens when there's a clear standard or best practice and someone simply didn't follow it. Not to deliberately challenge the status quo or to thoughtfully iterate a new strategic twist, but simply due to a lack of training, poor communication, or complacency. These are not failures that push innovation. But while they should not be celebrated, neither should they be shamed.

Instead, leaders should respond to preventable failures with clearer processes, additional support, and/or better systems.

Understanding these distinctions helps leaders respond appropriately and enables them to build a culture of bounded psychological safety—where clear expectations allow smart risks while still discouraging sloppy or avoidable mistakes. Not every mistake deserves a trophy, but not every failure is a red flag either.

Type of Failure	Characteristics	Action Required
Preventable	Repetition, careless errors, missed steps	Training, structure, oversight
Intelligent	Thoughtful experimentation with learning intent	Celebrate and scale learning

What Is a Failure Boundary and Why Does It Matter?

Failure boundaries create a sandbox for experimentation and play within your organization and your team. They define the outer edges of what's fair game to question, tweak, or even outright break. When teams know the hardline limits—whether related to compliance, safety, ethics, or budget—they can make bolder moves everywhere else. They don't waste energy second-guessing or worrying about stepping on the third rail. Instead, they focus their energy on solving problems creatively.

A clear failure boundary doesn't just permit risk; it invites it. It says, "Try it. Learn. We've got your back."

In 2009, when I founded my research and consulting company, Avenue M Group, times were rough all around. The United States was in the middle of the most severe economic downturn since the Great Depression. Though the recession technically began in late 2007 and ended in mid-2009, its ripple effects outlasted the initial crisis. Unemployment peaked at 10 percent. Banks stopped lending. Entire industries went into survival mode. For many businesses and associations, it was a brutal time to establish credibility, build a client base, access resources, and attract new members or conference attendees.

I built Avenue M Group to provide evidence-based insights and support to professional and trade associations. Having already worked at three associations, I was well versed in many of the challenges associations face, even during good economic times. During this downturn, high unemployment and deep budget cuts drove steep declines in association membership and meeting attendance. So, while they desperately needed to gather feedback on how best to serve members, many organizations lacked the means to fund the research.

If I wanted to build a client base and stay in business, I had no choice but to experiment with new pricing and delivery options. It was during this time that I came up with the concept of "Ten Terrible Ideas." Once a month, I would write down ten of the worst, most extreme ideas for attracting new clients. Once the list was complete, I had to flip the ideas into something I could actually test or try. For example, one "extreme" or "terrible" idea was to give away our research for free. The flipped version looked like this: We started out by offering two surveys for the price of one—a membership study and a post-conference evaluation study. While the bundling of two surveys for the price of one did bring in new clients, I knew we would eventually have to raise prices.

The broader economic downturn also created an unexpected kind of clarity. With fewer distractions and lower expectations for immediate success, I could focus on creating real value with what I had. I wasn't trying to scale fast. I was trying to solve problems that mattered to my potential clients. That mindset, along with the constraints I faced, shaped how I built Avenue M. It also reflected the essence of bounded psychological safety: I had room to try bold ideas, but I understood the boundaries—financial constraints, ethical standards, and client needs—that couldn't be ignored. I said "no" to distractions. I experimented. And most importantly, I gave myself permission to learn out loud, even when things didn't go as planned.

And I wasn't alone. Some of today's most recognizable brands were born in that same turbulent year: Airbnb, Uber, Slack, and Square. They didn't have the luxury of market certainty or excess capital. What they did have was a clear problem to solve and enough breathing room to try, fail, then get up and try again.

Recessions Shrink Resources but Expand Possibility

There's something counterintuitive about recessions: While they shrink access to funding and customers, they often expand what's possible. That's because downturns can force some big companies to retreat. They pause moonshot projects. They freeze hiring. They cut innovation budgets. Risk tolerance drops, and they get cautious.

This creates gaps in markets, in talent pools, and in customer attention for smaller, newer players to experiment. Suddenly, there are new, wide-open spaces for smaller companies, startups, and even nonprofits to explore, build, and test new ideas without getting outpaced or overshadowed.

In 2009, established brands in hospitality, transportation, and finance were cutting costs and focusing on core products. As major hotel brands struggled to trim spending fat without disappointing guests, Airbnb experimented with strangers sleeping on air mattresses. Meanwhile Uber tested a luxury black car app, and Square empowered artists and flea market vendors to take card payments with a dongle and smartphone. These were weird, unproven ideas. But no one was stopping them. Because in the absence of attention from the major hotel chains, constraints became creative fuel.

One of the most powerful insights from my research and firsthand experience is this: Constraints create clarity. In a downturn, you can't do everything. So, you prioritize. You can't afford to waste time. So, you experiment quickly. You can't afford to play it safe. So, you take intelligent risks. In doing so, you often create something more meaningful and more resilient than you would have in times of abundance.

Imagine if the competitors to these disruptive companies had embraced that same mindset. What if Hilton or Hyatt had created a division tasked with reimagining the hotel experience from scratch? What if Visa had built Square before Square did? What if a taxi company had given its customers real-time GPS tracking and instant driver reviews in 2009?

The truth is that most large companies don't fail because they lack ideas. They fail because they lack a culture that brings those ideas to the surface to be tested and iterated until they either sink or take off in a big, new way.

Innovation loves a vacuum.

When big companies retreat, opportunities open up. In a downturn, customers are more open to new solutions. Talent is more available. Attention is easier to capture. Experiments and bold ideas face less resistance.

A Culture of Safety Fuels Smart Risk-Taking

At the heart of this approach to brainstorming is a simple but powerful idea: Innovation thrives where failure isn't fatal. Where the goal isn't perfection, but progress. And where failure boundaries are clearly defined, not hidden, arbitrary, or simply defaulting to "what we've always done."

TEN TERRIBLE IDEAS:
A BRAINSTORMING TECHNIQUE

The Rules:

1. Set a timer for ten to fifteen minutes. Don't overthink it. The goal is quantity, not quality.
2. List ten or more outrageously bad, terrible, or extreme ideas you would never attempt or do. The more absurd the better. For example: "give everything away for free."
3. No judgement allowed. No idea is too ridiculous.
4. Once the timer goes off, flip each idea into a testable concept. "What's the non-absurd version of this idea?"
5. Pick a few to pilot. Design a small test and gather data.
6. Analyze and reflect on what worked and what didn't.
7. Repeat this exercise on a monthly or quarterly basis.

This technique works because it rewires your brain to explore without pressure. It normalizes failure as part of the process and helps uncover ideas you'd never get to if you only aimed for "good."

Want your team to be more creative? Try starting with the worst.

When you know the rules of the sandbox, you play better. You collaborate more. You speak up sooner. You iterate faster. And when something doesn't work, you don't hide it—you harvest the fruits of that failure for insight. That's the difference between a traditional team and an innovative one.

To build a culture like this

1. **Define the red lines clearly.** Get curious and be clear and specific. Ask, *What's nonnegotiable? What can be experimented with?*
2. **Celebrate efforts, not just outcomes.** Recognize the courage it takes to try.
3. **Normalize reflection.** Build in time to ask, *What worked? What didn't? What's next?*
4. **Create bounded psychological safety.** Let people know they won't be punished for smart, well-intentioned missteps—within clear, strategic constraints.

Questions for Leaders

- When was the last time your team was encouraged to try something bold?
- Do your employees know what kinds of risks are acceptable?
- Is there a safe space in your organization to share failures and lessons learned?
- Could you launch a "put us out of business" project—before someone else does?

Catching Mistakes Before They Happen

In high-stakes environments like healthcare, mistakes can have profoundly serious consequences. But errors are inevitable everywhere, even in hospitals. That's why the Good Catch Program at the Children's Hospital of Philadelphia (CHOP) has been so transformative. Nurses, doctors, and staff view mistakes not as shameful failures but as early warnings—valuable data points that can lead to safer systems and smarter decisions.

This mindset shift is the heart of the Good Catch Program, a proactive initiative focused on identifying and addressing potential issues before they cause harm. It's rooted in what's known as a "Just Culture,"[5] where individuals are not punished for making mistakes, but rather held accountable for how they respond to them. The focus is on learning, not blame.

To make the program work, CHOP embedded several key practices:

- **Training:** Staff learn how to spot and report near misses.
- **Accessibility:** The reporting system is quick and easy to use.
- **Recognition:** Employees who speak up are publicly celebrated.
- **Leadership:** Leaders model openness and respond with curiosity, not criticism.

In 2017, one such "Good Catch" led to hospital-wide changes that reduced the risk of patient accidents. A patient care assistant noticed that a hospital bed moved slightly, even though the brakes were on. The patient wasn't harmed, but the assistant brought it up during a daily safety huddle. Her observation led to an inspection and the discovery that 60 percent of beds had faulty wheel locks. Luckily, the issue got addressed before anyone could get injured.

In most companies, these small "catches" never make headlines. But what if they did? What if teams were trained, encouraged, and rewarded for raising their hands and saying, "Hey, something feels off"?

Attributes	CHOP Good Catch Program	Aviation Safety Reporting System (ASRS)
Industry	Healthcare	Aviation
Organization	Children's Hospital of Philadelphia	NASA (on behalf of FAA)

Attributes	CHOP Good Catch Program	Aviation Safety Reporting System (ASRS)
Who Can Report	All hospital staff	Pilots, air traffic controllers, flight attendants, maintenance crews
Reports	Near misses, safety concerns, potential risks to patients	Operational errors, near misses, safety hazards
Confidentiality	Yes	Yes
Primary Goal	Promote a culture of safety and learning	Improve safety
Outcome of Reports	Recognition and process improvements (innovation)	Systemic recommendations, policy changes

Case Study:
The Aviation Safety Reporting System (ASRS)

NASA, on behalf of the Federal Aviation Administration (FAA), developed the Aviation Safety Reporting System (ASRS) to give aviation professionals a confidential channel to report near misses, operational errors, and safety hazards. What makes ASRS especially powerful is its inclusivity: Pilots, air traffic controllers, flight attendants, and maintenance crews are all invited to submit reports. By empowering the people closest to daily operations to identify and communicate risks, the aviation industry has fostered a culture of safety grounded in transparency and learning.

Confidentiality is at the center of this program. Reporters are protected from punitive action, which encourages honesty without fear of retribution. The primary goal is not to assign blame but to uncover system vulnerabilities before they result in disasters. This psychologically safe environment not only boosts participation but also ensures that even minor concerns—what might otherwise be brushed off—get captured and analyzed.

Over time, ASRS has helped create systemic improvements.[6] Insights gathered from reports have led to revised flight procedures, enhanced crew communication protocols, and even policy changes at the federal level. Rather than relying solely on top-down regulations, ASRS represents a bottom-up innovation engine, proof that when front-line employees are trusted to share what they see, organizations can evolve with both safety and innovation in mind. (More on the role of how frontline employees can help organizations innovate in chapter 8.)

What Do Elephants, Dead Fish, and Vomit Have to Do with Psychological Safety?

In the early years of Airbnb's hospitality industry disruption, its leaders learned from an internal survey that employees had some key complaints about certain aspects of how the company operated. Airbnb's co-founder and Chief Product Officer Joe Gebbia wanted to create a company culture that emphasized transparency, focused on the customer, and embraced a learning mentality. So, they defined new company terms for employees to use when submitting feedback:

"Elephants" described major, delicate issues that everyone in the room avoids talking about. The big, obvious issues that everyone sees but no one brings up. Say, a broken process or a program that no longer delivers value but continues to drain resources. These are the kind of topics that derail innovation and lower morale when they go unaddressed. By giving them a name, Airbnb gave employees permission to drag (or maybe push) the elephant into the light and start a conversation about it.

"Dead Fish" were unresolved issues from the past, things that hadn't healed but still festered beneath the surface. It could be a product decision that alienated a team or an initiative that failed without proper closure. These events still shape employee trust and need acknowledgment before people could fully move on.

"Vomit" happens when employees share something that's bothering them, and they want to know that someone is listening—even if the complaint is "poorly digested." These weren't always well-articulated complaints. Sometimes, they were half-formed, messy, and uncomfortable. But they mattered, because they came from a place of genuine frustration or concern.

When you build a culture where people feel safe to speak up—and where leadership listens—mistakes become moments of insight. Near misses become new ideas. And employees stop playing it safe and start thinking boldly.

How to Let People Know Their Observations (and Missteps) Matter

1. **Create and communicate:** Identify and promote a variety of ways for employees to report concerns without fear of retribution.
2. **Recognize and reward:** On a monthly basis, collect and share stories or occurrences when individuals identified potential issues, reinforcing the importance of their contributions.
3. **Educate continuously:** Provide training to help employees recognize potential risks and understand reporting procedures.
4. **Lead by example:** Leadership should model the desired culture, demonstrating that safety and improvement are organizational priorities.

Redesigning the Edge

Innovation doesn't require unlimited resources. It requires clarity, curiosity, and the courage to lead differently. That's exactly what Kelleigh Shankel, chief technology officer (CTO) at Battle Motors, brings to the table. Her story and the transformation underway at Battle Motors embody three core ideas that run throughout this book: the power of listening to every voice, the freedom found inside constraints, and the boldness to take more shots.

Originally founded as Crane Carrier Company (CCC) in 1946, the Ohio company quietly built vocational trucks that powered the backbone of heavy industry for decades. But in 2021, Battle Motors, a leader in electronic vehicles, acquired, rebranded, and infused CCC with new leadership, capital, and direction. The company's mission shifted from designing and building vehicles for severe-duty applications to accelerating the transition to electric vehicles for fleets. Today, Battle Motors blends legacy manufacturing excellence with cutting-edge technology and a bold commitment to electrification.

This transformation wasn't just symbolic. Battle Motors expanded their acquisition's Ohio manufacturing facility from 125,000 to 325,000 square feet. A $120 million Series A funding round, followed by a $150 million Series B round, fueled product development. This included the launch of a Class 8 severe-duty electric truck, the proprietary RevolutionOS vehicle intelligence platform, and a Smart Cab system equipped with advanced safety features.[7]

In an industry known for complexity, regulation, and even resistance to change, Battle Motors positioned itself as a fast-moving force, and chief technology officer Kelleigh Shankel led much of that charge. Kelleigh's path to the CTO role is anything but conventional. As the youngest of four girls, she grew up playing in the garage with her dad, who gave her tools instead of toys. At sixteen, she became the youngest engineer ever hired at Ford Motor Company after a career-ending injury ended her dream to compete in the Sydney Olympics gymnastics events. Her early experience at Ford—a highly structured, high-volume environment—gave her a great start, but it also showed her the limits of legacy thinking.

So, when she arrived at Battle, she took a different approach.

"I brought on engineers who were tired of unnecessary constraints," she said. Instead of prescribing solutions, she asked questions. Instead of enforcing hierarchy, she created space. "With our interns, I said, 'Here's the problem. These are the lines we can't cross—safety and compliance. Everything else? Question it.'"

This is where the first principle comes into play: *Make every voice heard*. Kelleigh didn't just empower her most senior engineers—she empowered everyone, including the interns. That opened the door for real breakthroughs.

For example, they handed Daniel Nguyen, a co-op intern fresh from California Polytechnic State University, a dysfunctional EV cooling system to redesign. "It needs to cool the batteries, be safe, and be serviceable," she told him. "Everything else is yours."

Daniel delivered a modular unit now called the "power sled." It saved two hundred pounds, improved cooling efficiency by over 20 percent, and cut service time by more than ninety minutes. His work won two SAE International (formerly the Society of Automotive Engineers) engineering awards and his university's top capstone award. Battle hired him full-time.

That kind of innovation doesn't happen in command-and-control systems. It happens in cultures where every voice is heard, especially the ones people usually overlook due to lack of experience or seniority.

When You Have Nothing to Lose

Dan Chuparkoff, a former global product lead at Google, offered a fascinating lens into how innovation plays out differently across Alphabet's sprawling landscape. "People don't realize there isn't really a 'Google,'" he said. "Alphabet is a holding company that owns more than 2,000 unrelated organizations. Within that structure, the experience of innovation varies wildly."

In theory, you might expect the most successful teams, those responsible for products like Google Search or Google Cloud, to be the most innovative. After all, they have deep resources, top talent, and brand recognition. But in practice, the opposite is often true.

"Search hasn't fundamentally changed in years," Dan explained. "Google Cloud is third in the market. These teams have thousands of employees and too much at stake. They've become risk averse."

Now compare that to an internal team like Tables, a lesser-known startup housed inside Alphabet. "They had eight or nine people, incredible resources, and three years to figure it out or get fired trying," Dan said. "No customers. No legacy baggage. They could take as many shots as they wanted without fear of disrupting something big."

Another small Alphabet team, Checks, experimented with how companies write privacy policies, a dry but critical topic, and an area ripe for reinvention. These smaller, bounded teams had what the big ones didn't: room to experiment, fail, and try again. They operated with bounded psychological safety, having the freedom to fail, but always within clear, focused parameters related to time, resource, and team size limits.

Dan's insight echoes a critical truth about innovation: It doesn't thrive in limitless environments; it thrives where rules are well defined, and failure is both expected and accepted. That's the very definition of bounded psychological safety. Many people in organizations aren't looking to shake things up. They're trying to stay employed.

"I've been on all kinds of teams," he said. "There are always folks whose goal is not to innovate; it's to not get in trouble. They need clarity—what's allowed, what isn't. Without that, they freeze."

The most innovative environments aren't the ones with the fewest rules; they're the ones where expectations, support systems, and limits are all clear. Especially in large organizations, there's always a tension between the divisions tasked with minimizing risk (compliance, legal, finance) and those tasked with pushing boundaries (marketing, customer experience, R&D). Innovation happens in the space where those tensions are acknowledged and managed, where people are allowed to experiment and fail.

Across all of these industries, one theme emerges: The organizations that grow, adapt, and innovate are the ones that make it safe to speak up. Programs like CHOP's Good Catch and NASA's ASRS demonstrate that near misses and failures, when identified early and treated as opportunities to learn, can prevent major breakdowns (and maybe even lead to breakthroughs). Of equal importance, these programs create cultures where employees are actively engaged in making things better.

What I love about these programs is that they create a mindset—established at the top and carried throughout the organization—that prioritizes taking thoughtful risks, experimenting, and learning over "saving face" and casting blame. By creating reporting programs, recognizing contributions, and modeling curiosity over punishment, leaders can turn "intelligent mistakes" into a competitive advantage.

This completely changes how people show up at work. Instead of staying quiet, they speak up. Instead of playing it safe, they try new things. That shift happens in cultures of bounded psychological safety—where experimentation is protected but not limitless. At Intuit, giving out "Failure Awards" helped relieve pressure and encouraged teams to run small experiments without fear. At Airbnb, those quirky sounding

"Elephants, Dead Fish, and Vomit" sessions gave people permission to say the hard stuff out loud. And when they did, the company got better. It wasn't about complaining or blaming; it was about catching something early enough to fix it.

Failure doesn't have to be the opposite of success. It can be the path to it. Sometimes, it even draws the shortest line to innovation. Separating intelligent failure from careless error is the key.

When employees fear failure, they don't just avoid taking risks; they may also stay quiet about potential issues that could blow up. They may avoid sharing ideas that aren't fully baked but could turn into something. They will often default to what they've done in the past—what's worked before—even if they see signs that a changing market is craving something new.

If you don't work in a culture that embraces the role of failure or mistakes as the path toward innovation, you can adopt some micro-habits:

- After every new product launch, marketing campaign launch, or other initiative, ask, *What worked? What didn't?*
- Create a Slack channel just for #Experiments.
- Create a "If I could do it over" Slack thread.
- Conduct pre-mortem meetings to ask, *How might this fail?*
- Create an "Almost Brilliant" award. Recognize ideas that might not be complete failures but didn't produce the intended results.
- Rebrand "failures" as "findings" and keep a running log that anyone in the organization can access and contribute to.
- Create a "Dead Idea Cemetery" for ideas that failed but could potentially be exhumed and revived at a later date.
- Designate a week for "weird and wild" ideas. The weirder and wilder, the better.

- Collect and share stories of failures, near misses, and experiments from outside your organization that didn't succeed but became the basis for a new idea or concept.

Innovation doesn't happen when people have to walk on eggshells. It happens when they feel safe to try, safe to fail, and safe to share what they've learned. These kinds of programs don't just protect people or prevent issues. They build trust. They spark curiosity. And they help teams move faster and smarter.

If you want your organization to grow, adapt, and do work that really matters, start by making space for people to speak up, even when the outcome isn't perfect.

YOUR TURN TO THINK DIFFERENTLY

1. What systems could you create to help your team share near misses and lessons learned without fear of blame?
2. How might your organization's culture shift if you celebrated thoughtful attempts as much as successful outcomes?
3. What would an "intelligent failure" look like in your specific industry or role?

CHAPTER 6

You Said, We Did

What determines which organizations thrive amid change and which fall behind? In my decades of research and observation, I've observed some critical factors that can make all the difference. I've seen it with traditional brands, scrappy startups, well-known Fortune 100 companies, and global associations.

Here's the trick: If you want to innovate and stay relevant, you need to give people the opportunity to speak up—but that's just the start. What you do next matters much more. Because as a leader, it's your job to make sure they know that their voices matter. It's about creating a culture built on follow-through, where feedback fuels decisions and leadership is measured by action, not just intent.

When people share ideas, suggestions, or critical feedback, they are showing signs of trust. They're also taking a risk. They may doubt that their ideas matter to leaders, that they will be valued, or even that they will be understood. They may also be testing organizational leadership to see if they're really listening.

If their feedback goes into a black hole and receives no action or even acknowledgment, the result isn't just disappointment. It can shut down voices altogether. Snoozing on the suggestion box sends the message that the request for feedback is more performative than forthright. Over time, this leads to employee disillusionment, disengagement, or even attrition.

Creating a "You Said, We Did" culture isn't about placating people but rather showing that when you ask for suggestions and ideas, you're listening. And you're ready to respond. It's about making the value of their feedback visible.

That way, when organizations send out surveys, their teams don't simply delete the emails and ignore the requests. What we often call "survey *fatigue*" among workers but is actually a symptom of *survey inaction* among leaders. This occurs when you repeatedly ask for input but appear to do nothing with the information you gathered. Eventually, people stop bothering to share their thoughts and ideas.

Having conducted research with more than half a million people over the last fifteen years, I've observed that the greatest deterrent to collecting input from employees, customers, patients, or clients is not a lack of interest. Rather, it's the belief (right or wrong) that when opinions are shared, nothing happens. No actions are taken to implement suggestions or even acknowledge concerns.

Of course, you can't act on everything—and you don't have to. The real power lies in transparency. That means getting honest about what input you're seeking and closing the loop between listening and leading. People don't expect perfection, but they require respect, for both their time and their input. That respect shows up most clearly in what you do with the feedback you get.

Innovating: One Brick at a Time

A few years ago, I arrived at my older sister Debbie's California home— and immediately noticed that something was different. The photos that once lined the credenza—of our parents, the two of us hiking, and one of my daughter (her only niece)—had all been moved. Now, in their place, stood a nearly three-by-two-foot (thirty-three-by-twenty-two-inch) Millennium Falcon made entirely of LEGOs.

When we were growing up, I remember my sister building *Star Wars* models from sets, but this was a whole new level. As she gave me a tour of her growing collection of new LEGO builds, including Cinderella's Castle, Hogwarts, R2D2, and dozens of others, I realized this wasn't just a revived hobby. It was an essential outlet. A creative reset button.

As a senior director in finance at a large publicly traded company, Debbie spends a majority of her time developing budgets, making financial forecasts, and analyzing trends. She explained that building LEGO sets has become a way to decompress after work. It's meditative, tactile, and gives her a sense of accomplishment she can literally hold in her hands. Soon after completing her first few advanced builds, she discovered a Facebook group called *Ladies LEGO Lounge (and beyond)* and found something even more powerful: a supportive, like-minded community of women who build, troubleshoot, and cheer each other on. While the Ladies LEGO Lounge and other Facebook groups offer support to LEGO fans and customers, they also serve as a critical feedback tool for LEGO.

Debbie's new hobby, however, almost didn't happen. About a decade earlier, LEGO was teetering on the edge of bankruptcy. The company had lost focus, launching video games, theme parks, and a large product line that diluted its core. LEGO would come out with elaborate builds connected to movies and see a momentary spike in sales, but these generally failed to generate lasting interest in LEGO's basic products. At the same time, specialty toy retailers were declining, and online shopping was on the rise. Plus, less expensive versions of brick building toy kits began flooding the market. By 2004, LEGO was nearing crisis.

The eventual turnaround came from a fundamental shift in LEGO's strategy, simplified operations, getting back to the basics, and—most critically—listening to its customers.

In October of 2004, thirty-five-year-old Jorgen Vig Knudstorp stepped into the role of CEO at LEGO and proceeded to transform the company.[1] Much of this well-documented revival story leaned on direct customer feedback, combined with identifying necessary creative boundaries. In other words, LEGO not only identified the fence around their innovation playground but also asked customers how they wanted to play. Most importantly, they acted on that information.

Knudstorp reduced the development time for new products and created new ways to engage customers of all ages. One was the launch of the LEGO IDEAS platform, a website where anybody can not only share what they've made but also submit ideas to "become a LEGO designer." When I visited the site, the first thing I read was this statement:

> Love getting imaginative with LEGO bricks? Fancy yourself as a LEGO master builder? Well, this is the place to be. Share your cool creations and creativity, enter challenges, showcase your proposals for new LEGO Ideas sets and vote for awesome models dreamt up by your fellow fan designers.

Today, the LEGO Brand Framework includes catchphrases that promise:

- Play ("play well")
- People ("succeed and grow together")
- Planet ("positive impact")
- Partner ("mutual value creation")

LEGO encourages would-be set designers to start by checking for intellectual property conflicts, building their model, and uploading both photos and a short description. If approved, the submission gets published on the platform . . . but that's just the beginning. To move forward, the idea needs to gather ten thousand votes from other LEGO enthusiasts.

Once a consumer idea reaches that threshold, LEGO evaluates it for feasibility and market potential, among other things. If it makes the cut, the creator gets to collaborate with LEGO designers to turn the concept into a retail-ready set, available in stores and online. The platform has become a vibrant hub for innovation, featuring everything from a NASA spacecraft to a vintage typewriter. Fans aren't just buying LEGO sets; they're helping to co-create LEGO's future and contribute to the organization's innovation.

Debbie's later experience in the Ladies LEGO Lounge mirrors how people interact on LEGO IDEAS. This shows that success isn't just about knowledge, skill, or interest; it's about connecting with others. That Facebook group gives Debbie the boost to stick with something she loves, even when the builds get tricky. It offers a safe place to ask questions, contribute ideas, and be taken seriously. Research backs this up: Larger networks provide motivation and energy, while strong individual connections deliver richer feedback and smarter insights.

A study published in the *Journal of Global Information Management* identified two key types of support on the LEGO IDEAS platform: emotional and informational.[2] Emotional support is the cheer that keeps you going because someone liked your idea or left a kind comment. Informational support is the challenge, the kind that helps you improve your design, rethink your approach, or sharpen your concept. Both types are essential to sparking innovation.

What I didn't realize that day in Debbie's living room is that my sister has joined a global phenomenon. She's one of millions of Adult

Fans of LEGO (AFOLs), a passionate and growing community that's been around for more than thirty years. LEGO doesn't just acknowledge and support AFOLs; it actively collaborates with them. The company created a dedicated AFOL Engagement Team to listen, support, and collaborate with adult builders. Through programs like LEGO IDEAS, fans have helped bring to life some of the most beloved modern sets, including sitcom apartments and swirling tornadoes inspired by movie scenes. LEGO also launched the LEGO Ambassador Network, which connects adult fans through events, online forums, and fan media. Each registered group has a community ambassador who acts as a direct line between the fans and LEGO's internal teams.

LEGO went from struggling to adapt in the early 2000s to becoming one of the most resilient brands in the world with a loyal group of followers. Not by doing everything internally, but by building a collaborative future with direct input from its community. In so doing, they (and market observers like me) learned a few things:

Key Takeaways from LEGO

1. **Gathering and responding to feedback is not just about interpreting data.** Done right, it can inspire devotion. LEGO didn't just ask for feedback; they empowered fans to co-create the future of the brand alongside them. Witnessing the real-time impact of their input builds trust, engagement, and unmatched loyalty.

2. **Communities thrive when they're seen and supported.** From the AFOL Engagement Team to the Ambassador Network, LEGO built the infrastructure to listen, act, and elevate voices outside their corporate walls.

3. **Co-creation isn't a risk; it's a strategy.** Letting customers into your creative process can feel like losing control, but done right,

it can unlock innovation that no internal team could dream up on their own.

From Toy Bricks to Tech Teams

LEGO rebuilt its future midstream by creating platforms for listening to feedback and engaging its customers in the creative process. Meanwhile ATLiS, the Association of Technology Leaders in Independent Schools, has embedded this same practice into its very DNA. But instead of crowdsourcing toy concepts, ATLiS is committed to listening to the real-world needs of technology professionals who work in private schools.

When Christina Lewellen became the first full-time CEO of ATLiS in 2019, she wasn't stepping into a typical leadership role. The organization had been founded just a few years earlier by three technology directors who realized that independent school technology leaders needed a professional home. By the time Lewellen arrived, ATLiS was growing fast, transitioning from an entirely volunteer-driven model to one led by paid professionals. At that point, the board was still made up entirely of founders and early volunteers who remained highly active and deeply committed. Managing this transition, Lewellen understood, required careful listening, but she knew she couldn't rely solely on her board for insight.

"That can be an echo chamber," she told me. So, Lewellen hit the road. Literally. She began visiting schools. Not just once (as many CEOs do early in their tenure), but continuously. "What I recognized in those early days is that, given that technology changes quickly, there was no way I could stop doing my listening tour," she said. "The listening tour was permanent."

Lewellen found that student results had very little to do with, for example, whether kids had a Chromebook versus an iPad to do their work. "It was about creating learners that were independent and coached and overseen—but also encouraged. And they were flourishing through failure."

What Lewellen witnessed went far beyond academic performance. It was a transformation in how students approached learning itself. In environments where character and community were prioritized, students weren't just allowed to fail; they were expected to. Failure was reframed as normal, even necessary, part of the learning process. There were maker spaces and coding labs in the schools where students, many of them young girls in an all-girl school, were encouraged to build, break, and build again. The goal was to learn problem-solving skills, which required experimenting and trying new things—and failing. They weren't just learning to code; they were learning how to deal with setbacks, and how to support each other through the process. They were flourishing through failure.

In gathering anecdotes through school visits, Lewellen noticed repeating patterns of missed opportunities. For example, she saw that some ATLiS members had developed inclusive community initiatives at their schools, but they hadn't shared these insights and practices with other ATLiS members. One ATLiS member school had implemented inclusive software choices like the pronunciation tool, NameCoach, which helps teachers get students' names right. They also offered different learning platforms to meet various student needs.

To help connect the dots for other members, Lewellen gathered a team of school tech leaders to create the Community Building Framework for Technology Leaders. This gave professional members a language and structure for articulating their contributions to inclusion and belonging, among other topics.

Instead of using a traditional strategic plan, ATLiS designed a "living strategic map" that positions the organization as a resource, mentor, and expert. While a traditional strategic plan includes a fixed set of goals, objectives, and outcomes, and can be linear and rigid, a *living strategic map* is more dynamic, providing direction without defining how it must be done. Lewellen believes the map empowers her and her team to be more adaptive and respond to emerging needs.

The ATLiS map aims to serve at three levels: tech teams, whole schools, and the broader education industry. This three-part structure gives Lewellen the flexibility to pursue and share ideas she hears in the field, whether speaking at accrediting body conferences or creating new programming around emerging technologies like AI. It also allows Lewellen and ATLiS to listen more closely and respond more nimbly to member needs.

Lewellen recalls a time when teachers across the country felt overwhelmed by the speed and uncertainty of AI's arrival. Individual tech directors at member schools struggled to advise and support them, so the leaders at ATLiS did something it didn't typically do. They developed AI programming in the form of a one-day, in-person workshop—not for their tech leader members, but for teachers at the schools where these members served. The flexibility of ATLiS's strategic map, combined with insights from Lewellen's ongoing listening tour, enabled her to experiment with a new idea that provided timely and much-needed value to members.

One of the most innovative ways ATLiS turns listening into action relates to how it recognizes and elevates members. Lewellen discovered that many of the tech professionals she serves lack traditional paths to leadership within their schools.

"Those are middle-of-the-organization people that don't often get a lot of celebration," she noted. For example, some technology professionals in independent schools operate at the core of implementation but lack formal authority or a seat at the decision-making table. They have significant influence over day-to-day technology decisions but limited visibility at the school's leadership level.

Because this trend impacts many members and member schools, Lewellen and her team reimagined what leadership development and recognition could look like. They expanded the organization's Pillar Award program, opened self-nominations for board and volunteer roles, and restructured their governance model so that more people could serve—and be seen.

"We used to have two-year chairs," she told me. "Starting next year, we'll move to one-year chairs because we want more people to be able to put 'ATLiS Board Chair' on their resume."

In doing so, ATLiS has made leadership itself a member benefit. And that insight came directly from listening.

An important component of "You Said, We Did" culture is closing the loop on feedback. Many organizations struggle with this, especially when they can't act on everything they hear. Lewellen shared that, rather than relying solely on strategic plan updates or traditional announcements, she uses ATLiS's member magazine as a vehicle for storytelling and follow-through.

"We have several hidden columns," she said. "Spaces that, with intention, are all about that feedback loop of 'You guys said you needed this; here it is.' Or 'You didn't say you needed it and yet we observed it, and here it is.'" In ATLiS's case, "hidden" doesn't mean secret; it refers to intentionally embedded elements that quietly close the feedback loop, spotlight community members, and show how ATLiS leaders act on insights without providing a formal report.

ATLiS has used their magazine to address everything from AI trends to salary equity insights. In one issue, they reported that women tech leaders were closing the pay gap, but only if they sat on their school's leadership team. That data point sparked the launch of a coach-led leadership community for women in tech, tailored to help them secure that critical seat at the table.

Obviously, trust isn't built through surveys alone, nor through meetings, websites, board retreats, or even ongoing listening tours. It's built through what we choose to do after someone speaks up. In Lewellen's case, it's also built through how often we choose to show up in the first place.

Why Input Must Lead to Action

Whether you run a global brand like LEGO, an association, or a startup community, the principle is the same: People engage more often and more meaningfully when they see that their input leads to action. Feedback without follow-through doesn't just waste opportunities; it chips away at trust. And that's a risk no organization can afford.

Brad Feld, co-founder of Techstars and partner at Foundry Group, has spent his career helping startups grow, not just with capital, but by helping them set the right foundations to adapt and thrive. In our conversation, he was clear: Feedback without follow-through is worse than silence. What matters isn't just listening; it's how you respond.

Feld didn't shy away from calling out a common leadership failure: the performance of agreement without real intention to act. This often looks like smiling in meetings while internally disregarding what's being said. It's the classic *nod-and-duck*: appearing agreeable on the surface while quietly avoiding responsibility or hard decisions.

"I think it's really unhealthy for a leader to behave that way," he said, adding that this is especially true when clarity and trust are on the line.

One common constraint most startups face is funding. Many of the companies Feld invests in reach a point where they're making progress, but that progress is slower than expected—and without additional funding, leaders will need to face difficult decisions. Feld explained that companies can create a culture of trust among their leadership team by leaning into these constraints. He cited an example from Glowforge, a company in his investment portfolio that makes desktop 3D laser printers. In late 2023, the company faced a perfect storm: A major product launch coincided with a failed funding round, leaving the business nearly out of capital.

"We basically said, 'We'll fund this, but this is the last money,'" Feld recalled. Without additional financing options, the leadership team had to make some critical choices.

According to Feld, Glowforge's CEO, Dan Shapiro, didn't panic or deflect. Instead, he and his team chose to restructure internally, which meant laying off thirty employees—a significant portion of its workforce—and operating within the limited resources they had left.

"They did a restructure that was very aggressive," Feld said. The goal, he explained, was to develop a way to "never run out of money." That meant hard decisions, leaner operations, and a more intense focus. Fifteen months later, the original leadership team company was still intact, navigating challenges and thriving. What stood out to Feld wasn't just the survival of the company; it was the strength of their enduring leadership culture.

"The leadership team has hung together," he said. "It's very powerful to see a leadership team like that, that committed." Their success didn't come from having unlimited resources or flashy strategy slides. It came from aligned goals, clear communications, and a shared commitment to act decisively in the face of reality.

What makes the Glowforge story a strong example of "You Said, We Did" culture was how the leadership team responded not just to financial constraints, but to the concerns of their investors and their team. Shapiro didn't sugarcoat the situation or delay decisions; he communicated the urgency with clarity, laid out a path forward, and empowered his team to contribute to the solution. By setting firm boundaries—this was the last round of funding—and aligning around a common goal of cash flow positivity, the leadership team created the bounded psychological safety and operational focus needed to move quickly and cohesively.

Their actions sent a message: "We heard you. We're taking this seriously. And we're acting now." That transparency and decisiveness created alignment and trust, allowing the team not only to survive, but to lead with renewed purpose.

For Feld, trust begins with clarity. "If, as a leader, people can't look at you and understand what is fact or fiction, it then makes it very hard to define clearly what the boundaries are." When teams don't know what's real or where they stand, progress stalls. That's why Feld champions leaders willing to engage with difficult truths, hear tough feedback from him and the investors, and name what others avoid.

What struck me most about our conversation was Feld's insistence on creating cultures where people are invited to not only speak but to actually influence outcomes. His work as founding chair of the National Center for Women in Information Technology (NCWIT) reflects that commitment as well.

"If you want to be inclusive, be thoughtful about how to be inclusive of people with different talent and different skill levels and different voices." NCWIT is a community of more than 1,600 organizations— from K–12 to higher education and related industries—dedicated to providing access to critical knowledge and information. Its mission is to promote inclusion in the technology ecosystem through innovative programs and research.

In other words, hearing more perspectives isn't about checking boxes. It's about building better systems and better outcomes. But only if those voices are actually heard and their input acted upon.

None of this, Feld made clear, happens through words alone. "If the leader doesn't believe it's important, it won't happen," he said. "If you develop a reputation for being direct, being honest, being clear—and when you're wrong, owning it—that's very powerful."

A "You Said, We Did" Worksheet

1. **Where is our organizational feedback coming from?** List three to five sources of feedback you currently collect. Are you engaging employees, customers, clients, and members? Is there anyone not on the list who should be?

   1. ....
   2. ....
   3. ....
   4. ....
   5. ....

2. **What are we hearing?** Jot down three pieces of feedback that recently stood out (positive or critical). Use the actual words or themes they used.

   1. ....
   2. ....
   3. ....

3. **How are we responding?** For each example above, note your team's response—or lack of one.

Feedback	Response Given?	Action Taken	Communicated Back?
Example 1	☐ Yes / ☐ No	☐ Yes / ☐ No	☐ Yes / ☐ No
Example 2	☐ Yes / ☐ No	☐ Yes / ☐ No	☐ Yes / ☐ No
Example 3	☐ Yes / ☐ No	☐ Yes / ☐ No	☐ Yes / ☐ No

What patterns do you notice? Where are the gaps?

4. **How do we design—and close—our "you said, we did" loop?**
    Choose one piece of feedback to turn into visible action. Fill
    out the plan below.

    - **What was said:**
    - **What we're doing (or not doing):**
    - **Why (our rationale):**
    - **How we'll communicate this back:**
    - **Who owns it:**
    - **By when:**

One Size Does Not Fit All— a Global View of "You Said, We Did"

When it comes to acting on feedback, what works in one culture may
fall flat in another. The core idea may be universal: listen, respond,
and build trust. But the mechanics vary greatly.

How feedback gets shared and turned into action is shaped by
different industry needs, as well as deeply rooted cultural norms. In
some countries, transparency, rapid implementation, and public follow-
through are paramount. In others, discretion, quiet improvement,
and respect for hierarchy reign supreme. These differences aren't just
minor variations; they impact whether your efforts to engage truly
land or unintentionally backfire. Any global organization that wants
to foster trust, creativity, and inclusion across a diverse workforce
must understand these nuances.

In cultures that place a high value on hierarchy and group harmony,
direct feedback—especially if it's negative or confrontational—is
often avoided or outright discouraged. In these environments, silence

can speak volumes. Feedback may be delivered indirectly, but even when received, it's rarely acknowledged in public forums. Leaders are expected to interpret the subtle cues and make improvements behind the scenes. In these environments, asking for direct conversational input in private or small-group contexts will yield very little insight. Instead, leaders can more effectively gain information through anonymous, company-wide surveys. Framing feedback as a contribution to the collective good, rather than a personal critique, is key to encouraging participation.

By contrast, some organizational cultures operate with flat hierarchies, and employees expect to have a voice. These workers readily provide direct feedback, and they're more likely to expect a tangible, timely response. In such environments, transparency is nonnegotiable, and "You Said, We Did" isn't just a phrase; it's a promise. Leaders are expected to follow through and report back, whether through town halls, collaborative forums, digital dashboards, or internal newsletters. Closing the loop is more than a courtesy. It's a sign of basic respect.

Some years back, I partnered with the Association of Corporate Counsel (ACC) to lead a global research initiative examining work-life balance among in-house lawyers, particularly women and caregivers. There was growing interest in the topic, but little reliable global data. Organizations and law departments wanted to be more supportive, but they didn't fully understand what "support" looked like across different cultures, roles, and legal systems. So together, we designed and launched the *2014 ACC Global Work-Life Balance Report*, which captured insights from over two thousand in-house counsels across forty-one countries.

From the very beginning, it was clear that this wasn't just a quality-of-life issue; it was also a matter of career trajectory, retention, and equity. Fifty-five percent of participants said work-life balance was a major factor in their decision to take an in-house role, and one in four caregivers reported leaving a job that didn't support their caregiving responsibilities. Another 4 percent left the workforce entirely. Many respondents said they wanted to use benefits like telecommuting or flexible schedules but avoided them for fear of being passed over for promotions or seen as less committed. Perceived stigma often outweighed official policy.

The regional nuances were also telling. In North America, lawyers reported higher levels of satisfaction with their work-life balance than their peers, for example, in Asia, where longer hours made it harder to separate work from personal life. A respondent from the Asia Pacific region noted that although their company offered flexible work options, a "high performance" culture in the legal department meant those benefits mainly went unused. It's not that lawyers in Canada and the US couldn't relate. According to their feedback, those same benefits felt a bit more accessible to North American lawyers— but only when they also had support from their direct supervisors.

What made this project so powerful wasn't just the data. It was the impact of asking thoughtful, culturally sensitive questions and taking action on what they heard. This survey marked the start of a conversation about what it means to lead and support a global legal community. For many participants, the study itself felt like the first real signal that someone was listening.

In retrospect, this project became one of the clearest examples of a "You Said, We Did" moment. The ACC translated the feedback they gathered into boardroom conversations, policy reevaluations, and leadership training. They used the voices of their members to drive decisions.

That's how innovation begins, by listening to learn—and respond.[3]

Next Steps

1. **Audit your feedback loops.** Before you can improve how you act on feedback, you need to understand how you're collecting it. Map out every channel where feedback comes in: surveys, interviews, focus groups, emails, social media, customer support, one-on-ones with employees.

   Then ask, Are we actually using this input? Is it going anywhere meaningful? (For more clarity, complete the worksheet earlier in this chapter.)

   What you'll likely find is that some feedback channels are rich with insight but underutilized. Others might generate noise instead of clarity. A true "You Said, We Did" culture doesn't start with better answers; it starts with better questions about where your listening begins and ends.

2. **Make action visible.** People don't need every idea to be implemented, but they do need to know that someone heard them. Choose one piece of feedback from the past quarter, big or small, and make your response public. Highlight what was said, what you're doing (or not doing), and why. Transparency earns trust.

   Even if your response is, "We heard this, and we can't act on it right now," that honesty shows respect. The biggest mistake leaders make is staying silent. Silence too often gets interpreted as disregard. Visibility, even of thorny or delayed decisions, sends the opposite message: You matter, and your input is valued.

3. **Differentiate between listening and performing.** It's easy to host a town hall, issue a survey, or nod in a meeting. It's much harder to be changed by what you hear. Take a close look at how your team responds to tough or surprising feedback. Do you deflect? Delay? Or do you dig in?

Start by reflecting on a time when you received feedback that challenged your assumptions. What did you do with it? How did it shape your next steps? Leaders set the tone. When you move from defensive to curious, others will follow—and your culture will shift from performative listening to active, responsive learning.

4. **Build a feedback infrastructure.** LEGO didn't just stumble into community-powered innovation; they built systems specially designed for it. Take inventory: Do you have a person, team, or process responsible for managing and closing the loop on feedback? If not, start small. Designate one owner per feedback channel and give them a mandate to follow through.

   Over time, you can scale those efforts. Create dashboards. Launch a recurring "You Said, We Did" update. Celebrate people whose ideas made a difference. Feedback becomes fuel when it's operationalized. The goal isn't perfection; it's consistent, structured responsiveness.

5. **Customize your approach across cultures.** If your organization spans regions or countries, one-size-fits-all won't cut it. Start by learning the norms around feedback in each market where you operate. When is feedback given privately versus publicly? How do people expect responses? What role does hierarchy play?

   Then, adapt your systems accordingly. What works in San Francisco may fail in Singapore. Localization requires cultural fluency. When you respond in ways that reflect local norms, your efforts to build trust will land more deeply and drive real change.

   In the third and last part of the book, we'll explore why failure isn't just inevitable—it's invaluable. Because if "You Said, We Did" represents the first promise of trust, the second has to do with how you respond when things don't go according to plan.

YOUR TURN TO THINK DIFFERENTLY

1. What feedback have you recently collected that's sitting in a binder on the shelf or a file on your computer?
2. How could you make your response to input more visible and actionable to those who provide it?
3. If people consistently saw their voices lead to meaningful change, how might this help your organization overcome some of its challenges?

Part Three

Permission

CHAPTER 7

The Math of More Tries

I sat on an exam table in my physical therapist's office, dreading the next four words I expected to hear: "You can't run Boston."

The Boston Marathon is the holy grail for amateur runners. For me, it meant running 26.2 miles—about 26 miles farther than I'd previously intended to run over the course of my entire life—in under three hours and forty minutes. Yet there I was, three weeks out from the race, feeling like someone had taken a hammer to my knee.

After months of stretching my limits of strength, endurance, and discipline, I stood on the edge of what should have been one the biggest moments of my life. Now, all I could think was, *What if it all ends right here, in this room . . . before I even reach the starting line?*

Still, the craziest part of this moment was that I was there at all. For most of my life, I *hated* to run. With all my heart. In third grade, I got so good at negotiating my way out of running in Mr. Fry's gym class that my parents were convinced I'd grow up to become a lawyer.

At nine years old, I'd turned avoidance into an art form all its own. In an effort to find something that might stick, my mom launched what we now affectionately call *Operation: Find Sheri's Hidden Talent.* Over the next few years, she signed me up for piano, guitar, violin, trumpet, cornet, drums, and even harp lessons.

I quit them all. Sometimes after just two months.

I became an expert in quitting before someone could say I failed. I would frequently utter the words, "It's just not my thing," and move on. But the truth is, when things didn't instantly come easily to me, I quit.

After giving up on music, she signed me up for dance, gymnastics, and acting lessons—but my performing arts career peaked as a flying monkey in *The Wizard of Oz*. I never got a speaking part or kept up with choreography. As for tumbling, I could barely land a cartwheel. By the time I reached high school, we'd both given up on my "hidden talent."

The only activity I found any amount of success at was soccer—as our team's goalie, a position I earned through a combination of default and bargaining. Turns out, I was the only one willing to have balls kicked at her face—and only on one condition: that I didn't have to run laps with the rest of the team. By senior year, I was counting the days to when I would no longer be required to suffer through another gym class.

Fast-forward to my late twenties. I was single, living comfortably in Chicago, building a career and lifestyle blissfully devoid of running. Then, I start dating a runner. A real, race-entering, early-morning-miles kind of runner. Early on, I gave him *the talk*. "Just so you know," I told him, dead serious, "I will never run. Not even if we're being chased by bears."

But life has a way of surprising you. My aversion to running came to a screeching halt after a brush with mortality at age twenty-nine. What I'd thought was just indigestion turned out to be a football-sized tumor in my abdomen, complete with a blood clot near my heart. Overnight I went from an active, independent young professional to sitting on a hospital bed with a scary prognosis. When I woke up from surgery, the tumor and blood clot were gone. In their place, I'd gained the acute awareness that life doesn't always give second chances. That experience changed something fundamental within me.

I didn't want to be the person who quit everything anymore. I didn't want to sit on the sidelines of my own life. I wanted to try things, even if they were hard. Even if I wasn't good at them.

Even if I failed.

So, I started running. My first attempt was not even a mile. In fact, it was hardly a "run." More like a two-block shuffle from my Chicago apartment, on the corner of Sheffield and Wolfram, down to the Walgreens on Halsted. I definitely wouldn't call this run a success; it left me doubled over, struggling to catch my breath. But this time, I didn't quit.

Soon enough, I hit one mile. After finding a running club in my neighborhood, one mile turned into two, and two turned into five. When I ran my first race, I made every rookie mistake imaginable: bad shoes, worse pacing, nonexistent nutrition strategy . . . but I kept going.

I also set a goal: to eventually qualify for and run the Boston Marathon. To qualify, I'd have to first run a marathon in under three hours and forty minutes. I finished my first marathon in four hours and seventeen. Then 4:05. Then 3:53. Then 3:51. Then 3:47. Then 3:43.

Six marathons. Six attempts. And I was still falling short.

But each one taught me something. About fueling and pacing. About training and mental grit. I was shaving off minutes, gaining experience, and moving closer. Finally, at the Disney Marathon—a course not known for fast times or cool weather—I crossed the finish line in 3:39:35. I had qualified for Boston with just twenty-five seconds to spare.

The same person who once negotiated her way out of gym class and would rather take a soccer ball to the face than run laps had just earned a bib to the most prestigious (non-Olympic) marathon in the world.

But then, while training for Boston, I injured the iliotibial band near my knee . . . which brings us back to the physical therapist's office. As I sat on that table waiting for the therapist to tell me my Boston dreams were over, I began to realize just how far I've come—and that this story wasn't about running. It was about the math of more.

Specifically: more tries.

The distance between "I hate running" and "I qualified for Boston" isn't measured in miles. It is measured in *attempts*. In starting lines that I dragged myself to through sheer force of will. In finish lines that didn't go my way. In short, it was measured in failures—and in my willingness to keep going anyway.

The Real Equation for Success

We love overnight success stories. The struggling actor who finally got their big break, the underdog startup that sold for millions, the TEDx speaker with the viral talk. But what we don't see are all the reps behind those wins: the failed auditions, the flopped pitches, the many, many rejections.

There's a reason so many innovators and creators talk about failing: failing fast, failing forward, failing early and often. They understand that each failure is a step toward getting it right. If you study creative professionals, whether photographers, musicians, or inventors, you'll find that the most successful ones aren't necessarily the most talented. They're often the most prolific. The most stubborn.

The ones who take more shots.

As a photographer, I often take ten thousand photos for every one shot that makes it into a book or keynote. In the field, it's not uncommon to take thirty frames a second, to spend hours photographing the same hummingbird as it dives in and out of view. You don't always know in the moment which photo will be "the one." But you do know this: If you stop hitting the shutter, you'll miss it.

That same lesson applies to anything creative, risky, or bold. Want better ideas? Generate more of them. Want a stronger voice? Speak up more often. Want to make a difference? Be willing to try and try again.

Innovation Born from Failure

"Fail hard. Fail fast. Fail often." These words serve as a mantra and daily reminder for Battle Motors Chief Technology Officer Kelleigh Shankel as she navigates the rapidly changing world of high-performance, custom-engineered vocational trucking.

You will remember from chapter 5 that Battle Motors manufactures heavy-duty electric and diesel trucks used for essential services like waste management, construction, and short-haul logistics. These vehicles must perform flawlessly in punishing environments, meet evolving regulatory standards, and increasingly, deliver zero-emission performance.

Due to strict compliance and safety regulations, Shankel must assemble and lead a team of engineers who can experiment and innovate within these boundaries. According to Shankel, that shift in mindset toward greater experimentation can be hard at first, especially for engineers trained to stay within the lines.

"But once they get it," she shared, "they realize that some constraints are self-imposed. That's where innovation happens."

One of the clearest examples of this approach came from Daniel Nguyen, then a Cal Poly co-op intern at Battle Motors. Returning to that earlier example, when Shankel handed Daniel that problematic EV cooling system, she was challenging previously established industry standards. Shankel saw the value in giving every member of the team the space to explore alternative methods to achieve powerful results. As you'll remember, Daniel Nguyen's design would be far more efficient than anyone expected and go on to win multiple awards, top honors at his university, and a full-time position on the team.

As Shankel put it, "That's what happens when you give people room to challenge old assumptions."

But innovation isn't just about inventing new components; it's also about unlearning old, outdated habits. Shankel explained that

Battle works within legacy systems where "we've always done it this way" has become the default response. To tackle that, she approaches change management like a strategist. She observes what motivates each team member and stakeholder, tailoring her leadership to help them rethink outdated assumptions.

"Once someone realizes they're stuck in a thirty-year-old script," she said, "you can break that pattern and let them shine." For Shankel, innovation often starts with the courage to rewrite the rules. And that can involve some risk.

A philosophy that shows up in everything Shankel does can be summed up in the words she learned years ago from a mentor: "The best leaders take the heat and spread the warmth." In an industry that faces multiple constraints but must continuously innovate, Shankel leads with curiosity, the drive to make things better, and plenty of heart.

The Culture of One-and-Done

Despite the grown-up advice to "just do your best," many of us were conditioned to avoid failure. Many of us watched those same grown-ups self-criticize and decided to play it safe. Meanwhile, we also idealized the superstar actors and MVP athletes. We grew up chasing grades and trophies, believing our worth was tied to our wins.

As adults, we've carried that into our personal and professional lives. When something doesn't go well, we retreat. We assume failure means that we don't have what it takes, that our efforts and ideas just aren't good enough. But, more often, failure just means we haven't yet found the right formula, put in enough reps, or taken enough shots.

This dynamic plays out every day in organizations around the world. A team floats a new idea, tries a pilot, sees mixed results—and pulls the plug. The board backs a new strategy . . . but then, just one underwhelming quarter later, they revert to the old way. We treat innovation like a vending machine: *insert effort, expect outcome*. But real growth doesn't work that way.

Real growth looks more like training for your first marathon, then trying to qualify for Boston. It won't happen right away. You have to be willing to put in the miles. Willing to sweat, struggle, and fail—repeatedly and sometimes painfully.

Above all, to keep showing up again anyway.

Thirteen Failures That Inspired Success

Every morning, I'm gently nudged awake by a soft sound coming from my Alexa Echo Spot (whom I've affectionately renamed Ziggy). With a simple voice command the night before, I can set a specific wake-up time, choose the tone, and even get a morning temperature report. It's a modern convenience I've grown to love, not just because of its ease, but because it allows me to leave my iPhone charging in another room. That small shift has eliminated the constant distraction of late-night notifications and helped me reclaim more restful sleep.

The Amazon Echo, which has sold millions since 2015, owes its success to one of Amazon's bigger flops, the Fire Phone. The Fire Phone failed due to its poor app support and a clunky interface. Ultimately, Amazon had to write off the $170 million project and discontinue production.

But the failure wasn't a waste. Amazon's Lab126, which had developed the Fire Phone, leaned into what Amazon does best: voice, cloud-computing, and convenience. The Echo, equipped with Alexa, focused on intuitive interactions and real-world applications. Users can check the weather, play music, or ask it questions using only their voice. Engineers applied lessons learned from the Fire Phone's shortcomings to the Echo, improving on the strengths of that earlier model, while also emphasizing customer needs and ensuring broad developer support.

Other product failures that have been tied to future product successes include the following:

1. **Apple Newton:** Inspired iPhone/iPad touchscreen interface.
2. **Google Wave:** Failed collaboration tool that influenced Google docs and Gmail.
3. **Microsoft Zune:** Taught lessons for Xbox music and streaming services.
4. **Windows Phone:** Informed Microsoft's cloud-first strategy.
5. **Segway PT:** Commercial failure that advanced robotics applications and delivery bots.
6. **Arch Deluxe (McDonald's):** Upscale burger failure that refined McDonald's core brand.
7. **E.T. Atari game:** Prompted better quality control in the gaming industry.
8. **Textured wallpaper:** Led to the creation of bubble wrap.
9. **Tucker 48:** Failed car company that inspired safety innovations still used today.
10. **Google Glass:** Led to successful enterprise AR applications.
11. **Sega Dreamcast:** Ahead of its time with online gaming features.
12. **Friendster:** Early social network that paved the way for Facebook.
13. **MoviePass:** Unsustainable business model that proved demand for subscription services.

Each of these failures provided valuable lessons about technology limitations, market timing, consumer behavior, or business models that informed later successful innovations. But learning from failure isn't just reactive; it's also cultural. It's about building an environment where experimentation is expected, iteration is embraced, and stagnation is the real threat.

That's where Amazon's Day 1 philosophy comes in.

Amazon's Day 1 Philosophy

Imagine if your team always approached innovation with the same level of excitement, urgency, and focus as they do on the very first day of a brand-new project. Jeff Bezos strongly believes this is one of the keys to innovation. That's why he built what he calls a "Day 1 culture" at Amazon. In 2016, Bezos wrote a letter to shareholders outlining this philosophy: "Day 2 is stasis. Followed by irrelevance. Followed by excruciating, painful decline. Followed by death. And that is why it is always Day 1."[1]

At Amazon, this Day 1 mentality drives innovation and ensures the customer remains at the center of everything. In contrast, the way Bezos describes the "Day 2 mindset" reflects what can happen when an organization matures and scales. As growth continues, the focus often shifts from the customer to the company, which can bog down the initial excitement with complex internal processes, structure, and bureaucracy. This leads to slower decision-making and a gradual shift away from the customer.

Day 2 doesn't actually happen overnight (despite the misleading name). It occurs slowly over time, disguised as minor changes. On their own, these changes may not seem alarming, but collectively, they can lead to stagnation. Avoiding this slide requires a commitment to "Day 1" values, like challenging the status quo, relentlessly focusing on customers, and designing and using systems that support experimentation and adaptability.

"One thing I love about customers is that they are divinely discontent," Bezos wrote in his 2017 Letter to Shareholders. "Yesterday's 'wow' quickly becomes today's 'ordinary.'" Customers can provide endless ideas and inspiration to innovate, and their needs and desires will drive you to invent on their behalf.[2]

At Amazon Web Services, nearly 90 percent of the features they roll out are based directly on what customers ask for. The other 10 percent comes from listening and understanding how to anticipate customers' needs, based on their feedback and market trends.

According to Bezos, maintaining Day 1 requires five essential elements:[3]

How to Promote a Day 1 Mentality:

1. **Embrace true customer obsession.** Don't play coy. Get excited—even obsessed—about how you serve your people. Genuine passion empowers employees and leaders to stay curious while focusing on external issues, not internal ones.

2. **Resist proxies.** When you start looking internally, you can easily get distracted by policies, procedures, or processes—in other words, on proxies that can distance your team from taking risks.

3. **Embrace external trends.** Companies don't control the pace of change; they only control how quickly they can anticipate and respond to those changes. Instead of resisting the growing demand for cloud infrastructure, for example, they doubled down.

4. **Use high-velocity decision-making.** When a decision is reversable, or as Amazon calls it, has *two-way doors*, decisions should be made quickly with more focus on learning and less on launching something that's perfect. Whenever possible, avoid decisions that must be made by larger groups within an organization. "Death by committee" is a real phenomenon. The need for consensus often kills innovation. That's why Amazon favors small, empowered-teams (two-pizza teams they call it).

5. **Prioritize long-term, sustained value.** This requires a reinvestment in efforts over short-term profits and a willingness to be misunderstood. A decision may not make sense to everyone, and that's okay.

Amazon's Day 1 culture reminds us that staying innovative requires intentional discipline, not just early enthusiasm. But while Amazon emphasizes urgency and customer obsession as fuel for innovation, there's another ingredient that's just as critical: repetition.

Innovation isn't a one-time breakthrough; it's a habit. That's where practice comes in. Just like athletes or musicians, innovators and leaders need space to try, fail, and try again—not in the spotlight, but behind the scenes. Moving from a Day 1 mindset to a practice mindset means building systems where experimentation is the standard.

Practice as a Mindset

There's a reason why athletes and musicians practice more than they perform. Practice isn't about perfection. It's about volume of experimentation. It's about building muscle memory and resilience. It's about asking the right questions:

- *What if we treated leadership and innovation the same way?*
- *What if we created spaces where people could take more shots—and not just safe ones?*
- *What if teams were not measured just by outcomes but also by attempts?*
- *What if every team member's performance review included questions like, "How many ideas did you try this year? How many experiments did you run?"*

This doesn't mean perfection. It means shifting our mindset toward persistence and experimentation.

When you try something and it doesn't work, you haven't failed. Not if you've collected information and learned something valuable. Now you have data and insights you didn't have before. That might not be the win you want, but it can help set you up for it. Not every experiment needs to be a moonshot. It could be as minor and low-risk as changing how you onboard a new employee, tweaking the copy of your email marketing campaign, or finding a new way to respond when a customer has a complaint.

That's the thing about practice—it prepares you not just for the perfect day but for the unpredictable one. The one where conditions aren't ideal or the best-laid plan falls apart. Practice builds the kind of resilience that allows you to keep going anyway. It teaches you how to adapt, pivot, and trust the work you put in. Even when the outcome looks different than you first intended.

. . . Which brings me back to Boston, and that physical therapist's office.

Back to Boston

So, what *did* my physical therapist say to me that day I sat in her examination room, three weeks before my would-be Boston Marathon debut? After bracing myself for the worst possible news, I was thrilled when she started talking not about *whether* I could run the race—but *how*.

She told me I would need to run Boston differently than I had run other races. I'd need to adjust my pace, prepare for a slower time, and listen to how I feel—in other words, to not push through the pain. She knew that I wanted to keep running after this race and that I shouldn't try to "leave it all on the course," as some coaches are known to say before a big race.

I listened to her advice and ran that Boston Marathon. Not at the pace I originally wanted. Not with the ease I'd imagined. But I ran it. I crossed that finish line and soaked in every step, every loud cheer from the crowd, and the overwhelming feeling of finishing something I had started.

That race wasn't about speed. It was a celebration of all the attempts that came before it.

And that is the math of more tries. You don't get there by being perfect. You get there by not quitting.

Help Your Team Embrace the "Math of More Tries"

1. **Value the effort, not just the outcome.** It's easy to believe that success belongs to those who are naturally gifted or who always get things right on the first try. But more often than not, real achievement is born out of persistence: showing up, trying again, and refusing to give up.

   My journey to Boston wasn't about one race. It was about a series of missteps, small improvements and adjustments, setbacks, and even a few disappointments. Each marathon taught me something new and inched me closer to my goal. Success didn't come from a single breakthrough but from the accumulation of effort, including multiple failures.

   This mindset can be difficult to embrace, especially in a world that celebrates quick wins and instant gratification. We're often conditioned to believe that if something doesn't come easily, it's not meant to be. But that narrative discounts the transformative power of persistence. Whether you're training for a marathon, launching a product, or trying to lead a cultural shift in your organization, progress is rarely linear. Expect setbacks and plateaus.

   When you value effort enough to make it part of your team's success metrics, you will build a culture that learns, adapts, and iterates its way to successful outcomes.

2. **View failure as data collection.** Instead of treating failure as
    the verdict—the response to an effort—view it as an opportunity
    to further your knowledge and collect meaningful data. Failure
    tells you what works and what doesn't, what needs adjusting,
    and what needs to be explored further. Although many of the
    product flops and failures listed in this chapter didn't end in
    success, they did lead to insights that helped build other prod-
    ucts. To unlock the value of failure, it needs to be normalized
    within your organization.

    Kelleigh Shankel's work at Battle Motors demonstrates
    this beautifully. By giving her team room to fail within defined
    parameters, she ensures they're always learning, iterating, and
    evolving. Even their setbacks become sources of insight that
    inform the next breakthrough.

3. **Put in the reps.** No one expects someone to master a musical
    instrument or to become a world-class athlete after the first
    lesson, or even after the first year or two. We all know that it
    takes many years of hard work and practice to achieve success on
    stage or in the field. For real growth, embrace this same mindset.
    The more you practice, the more you refine your knowledge.

    You need to build your innovation muscle. Repetition helps
    you notice patterns, test variables, and see what doesn't work.

4. **Build a "try again" culture.** I often see companies shelve new
    ideas if they don't immediately succeed. Instead of having a
    one-and-done approach, create a culture that builds innovation
    into the budget, timing, and evaluation process—and vice versa.

    To build this kind of culture, leaders need to model resil-
    ience. This means sharing stories of failure, acknowledging
    when something didn't go as planned, and inviting others to

do the same. It also means creating structures that support experimentation. A failed pilot shouldn't be a career risk; it should be a springboard to the next version. As Shankel shared, innovation sometimes begins when people realize they're stuck in a thirty-year-old script. Give them permission to write a new script. It might introduce just the plot twist you need to make progress happen.

When organizations adopt a try-again mindset, something powerful happens: people stop fearing failure. They start seeing it as part of the process. They take more risks, speak up more often, and pursue bolder ideas. Over time, those attempts add up. That's the math of more tries, not just in personal growth or physical endurance, but in every workplace that dares to believe in the value of trying again.

The first attempt is only the first step. It takes courage to put something out there, to create a new product or service to fill a gap and drive market demand. Building a life, a team, or an organization that encourages and rewards repeated effort? That takes something deeper: a commitment to making risk-taking part of the culture. Understanding the math of more tries requires an appreciation of the sheer volume and grit it takes to push through.

Next, we'll talk about what makes that math sustainable. Because persistence alone isn't enough. If the leaders and systems around you still punish failure and only reward success stories, people will stop trying. To build momentum and resilience at scale, we have to make risk-taking a habit, not an exception.

So . . . how do we do that? What does it look like to create a team or organization where people don't just feel safe to take risks, but are expected to do so? Where failure is debriefed, not buried? Where new ideas are given room to breathe, stumble, evolve, and thrive? That's where we're headed next.

YOUR TURN TO THINK DIFFERENTLY

1. What would you attempt if you knew that "failure" was simply data collection for your next iteration?
2. How could your organization shift from measuring success to measuring persistence and learning?
3. What dreams or goals have you abandoned too quickly? What would "one more try" look like?

CHAPTER 8

The Frontline Fix

When we moved into a new neighborhood last year, one of my first priorities was finding the perfect local coffee shop. I narrowed it down to two within a mile of our house and visited both. I was also looking for a friendly staff and lines that weren't too long at the time of day when I would be stopping in for a cup of coffee.

After trying both coffee shops, I settled on the one within walking distance. One day I ordered my usual, an Americano with room for cream, medium temperature. When they called my name to pick up my drink, I took one sip and realized it was extra hot.

When the barista saw me wince, she immediately apologized and told me this happens frequently. But, she said, she had an idea: She would start adding either an "M" or an "H" at the top of the cup, indicating if the temperature should be medium or hot.

There was no manager she needed to call. No form to fill out. No multi-step protocol to log a complaint. She had the authority to fix the problem—and experiment with a solution—in real time.

The next time I came into the coffee shop, a different barista was working, and she immediately wrote the letter "M" on my cup after I placed my order and shared my preferred temperature. She also delivered the perfect cup of coffee at the right temperature. And right next to the register was a small sign that read, "Tell us how you like your drink. Our new letter system helps ensure we get it right."

That one tiny, unofficial change turned into a micro-innovation. All because a single frontline employee saw a pattern, took a risk, and decided to test a solution—without having to ask permission.

Yes, there was a risk in letting her do that. Maybe it wouldn't have worked. Maybe it would've confused the team. But here's the thing: If we want to innovate faster, improve customer satisfaction, and create a culture of responsiveness, we have to be willing to put decision-making into the hands of the people who are closest to the customer, even if there is a risk of failure.

This chapter is about organizations that do exactly that. Places where autonomy isn't just a value but a daily practice. It's about what happens when you trust people on the front lines to fix what's broken, try what's new, and improve what's possible. It doesn't always take a grand strategy. Sometimes, it starts with a small letter "M," a better cup of coffee, and empowering the frontline workers to experiment when they see a problem.

A Different Kind of House Call

In 2006, Jos de Blok, a nurse in the Netherlands, came up with a new way to deliver healthcare. De Blok believed that nurses, when trusted and supported, could deliver better care at lower cost. His solution was radical in its simplicity: flatten the hierarchy. He calls his model *buurtzorg*, Dutch for "neighborhood care."

Buurtzorg operates through small, autonomous teams of up to twelve nurses. There are no layers of middle management. Each team handles its own hiring, scheduling, budgeting, and caseloads. A back office of around fifty staff supports more than ten thousand nurses globally. If a team needs help, they can reach out to a regional coach, but decisions stay at the local level.

That autonomy does more than reduce bureaucracy. It allows frontline professionals to spot patterns, make changes, and test ideas without waiting for permission. It builds a foundation of trust where calculated risks feel safe, and innovation isn't relegated to a department; it's part of everyone's role.

In many organizations, risk-taking is often considered with large initiatives, venture investments, or top-down mandates. At Buurtzorg, it's embedded in everyday actions, like a nurse deciding to experiment with family caregiver schedules or design a tailored mobility plan before involving external professionals. The organization trusts its people to figure things out, and that trust isn't just symbolic—it's operational.

Because some of the most meaningful innovations didn't come from the top; they came from inside the teams. One such idea emerged when a physical therapist joined Buurtzorg after working in the UK. Inspired by what she saw, she began asking questions: *What if nurses, PTs, and OTs didn't work in silos? What if they teamed up from the beginning, delivering care collaboratively—in the home, in real time?*

In most healthcare systems, physical and occupational therapists are brought in late, after long delays and layers of approvals. This physical therapist had seen firsthand how this slowed recovery and increased long-term needs. So, she did what Buurtzorg empowers every team member to do: She acted.

Rather than seek permission from headquarters, she proposed a pilot directly to two local teams. They agreed. Together, they launched an experiment, inviting a PT and OT to work alongside the nurses, not outside the circle of care.

No waiting lists. No bureaucratic lag. If a nurse noticed early signs of a fall risk, the PT could intervene immediately. If a client needed home modifications, the OT could make recommendations that same day. The team didn't need to schedule long meetings. They made decisions around kitchen tables, alongside the client.

They called it Buurtzorg+. It started as a pilot. But like many ideas born from trust, autonomy, and a willingness to try, it didn't stay small for long.

Without hierarchy, nurses become entrepreneurs in care delivery. And this new model puts patients and their environment at the center of their caregiving decisions. The health professional considers their home environment and their network of friends, family members, and neighbors. Self-managing teams of twelve take care of individuals within a neighborhood. They meet the local occupational and physical therapists and other healthcare providers. The team makes decisions related to schedules, shared responsibilities, and referrals.

Buurtzorg's innovation-by-trust model doesn't just *sound* good; it works. A KPMG study[1] found that Buurtzorg teams were able to reduce client care hours by nearly 50 percent, while improving outcomes. Overhead costs fell to 8 percent, compared to an industry standard of 25 percent. And because clients regained more independence, nurses were able to serve more patients with fewer resources.

The organization has repeatedly been named "best employer" in the Netherlands by the Dutch magazine *Intermediar*, and its model has now been adapted in more than twenty-five countries.

Key Takeaways from Buurtzorg

1. **Empowered front lines spark innovation.** Those closest to the client or customer may have the best insights on how to solve a problem. *Let them.* They notice patterns leadership never sees because they're the ones living the details every day. When you give them permission to act on those observations, you turn complaints into opportunities and delays into real-time solutions.

Innovation doesn't always require a brainstorming session or a strategic plan. Sometimes, it just requires not getting in the way. The best ideas often surface when people feel both trusted and responsible to make things better.

2. **Small experiments can scale.** That's true whether it's a single letter on a cup of coffee or a trial run using PTs and OTs earlier in care plans. Both started as small-scale, low-cost experiments. By encouraging experimentation at the micro level, organizations can create a culture that embraces experimentation as part of their process to evolve, innovate, and better meet the changing needs of its clients or customers.

3. **Decentralized decision-making speeds innovation.** By removing the layers of bureaucracy and allowing individuals and teams to experiment with a new idea as soon as they see an opportunity, a company can learn and iterate quickly.

Questions to Identify Barriers to Frontline Innovation

1. **Where are the patterns?** Think of a recent customer complaint or a recurring issue. What was it? How often does it happen? Describe it in one sentence. (If nothing comes to mind, ask your team to record complaints or calls for the next month.)

2. **Who is the closest to this problem?** Think frontline staff, support reps, technicians, or customer service reps.

3. **Have those closest to the problem been asked for ideas?** Yes or no? If not, ask them.

4. **What's one small change a frontline team member could test without approval?** Where are the boundaries of what's

acceptable to change? Examples might include how something is labeled, offered, communicated, or delivered.

5. **What's the worst-case scenario if the experiment fails?** Is it reversible? Is there a reputational or financial risk associated with the experiment?

6. **What's the best-case outcome if it succeeds?** Could it improve satisfaction, speed, efficiency, or moral?

A Worksheet for Assessing Frontline Autonomy

Individually or in teams, rate the following on a scale of 1 to 5 (1 = strongly disagree, 5 = strongly agree).

- Our frontline teams feel trusted to solve problems in real time.
- We actively invite ideas and feedback from staff at all levels.
- Small-scale experimentation is part of our culture.
- It's safe to try, fail, learn, and try again.
- Decision-making is decentralized when it makes sense.
- Our team knows where the boundaries are for trying something new.

Which item scored the lowest? Why? What would it take to increase that score by one point?

What's your version of the letter "M" on the coffee cup? What's one thing your team could try this week to improve customer or client experience—without needing a full plan or permission?

Have you asked your frontline team?

Quick Tip to Get Started

Commit to identifying and trying a small experiment within the next seven days. Schedule a ten-minute debrief to share what worked, what didn't, and what to try next.

Empowering frontline employees doesn't require a big plan, just a starting point. The ripple effect of even a small gesture can be profound. I've seen it happen in boardrooms, at the doctor's office, at the dry cleaners, and coffee shops. Sometimes the biggest shifts begin with a tiny experiment and a team that feels trusted to run with it.

A Surprise That Sparked a Movement

Years ago, I worked as the chief marketing and membership officer at the Association Forum. Like many membership organizations, we faced an increasingly common problem: getting members to renew on time.

Our traditional renewal reminders, which included letter campaigns outlining the top ten reasons to renew and mailed invoices, were becoming easier to ignore. People were busy, and I believed they simply tossed or overlooked my carefully crafted campaign pieces. Every week that passed without a renewal meant more money spent on printing, postage, and staff time.

I needed to try something different.

So, I came up with a small experiment: I removed the letter and just sent a single-page invoice. Once someone renewed, we mailed them a plastic gift card. Not a coffee shop card or a Visa debit card. This was an education gift card that could be used toward any of our half-day professional development programs.

The accompanying message read, "We know times are tough and budgets have been cut. Thank you for renewing. Please enjoy a half-day educational program on us!" It was meant to be a small, unexpected "thank you."

As soon as the cards went out to the members who renewed during the first month of the campaign, word got out. People called and emailed my team. They shared the card with coworkers, posted about it on LinkedIn—and just like that, word of mouth did what no multi-touch campaign could: Renewals doubled compared to the same period the previous year. One member even wrote us a thank-you note, saying the gesture made her feel "seen and valued" in a way she hadn't expected.

Like any experiment, we hit a few snags. Some members lost the card (and the perceived benefit it delivered). Others never used it. And for us, this was a missed opportunity. Not because of the sunk cost (adding one more person to a program didn't cost us anything), but because our research showed that if a member attended just one program, they were significantly more likely to register for another and renew again the following year. Attendance wasn't just a perk; it was a predictor of retention.

That's when the power of my front line kicked in.

Our member service reps started fielding calls and emails from members who had lost their cards or missed the deadline to use them. And instead of escalating the issue to me, they solved it. They didn't ask for permission—they simply acted, because they understood the intent behind the program and felt empowered to deliver on it.

Why? Because I had already empowered them to spend up to $250 to "make things right" for any member, no questions asked. They knew the parameters, they understood the goals, and they acted. They issued new card numbers to anyone who lost their card. They allowed members to transfer the card to anyone in their organization, even a nonmember. This surprised our members.

When our service reps told me what they'd done, I didn't shut it down. Instead, I updated the rules and formalized it. Gift cards officially could be transferred to others and replaced if lost. The honor system would be enough. It would generate the goodwill and buzz I was looking for—and it worked.

Attendance spiked. Program participation increased significantly year over year. And when we surveyed program attendees, 100 percent of respondents who used the gift card said they would not have attended the program if they'd had to pay for it out of their own pocket.

What started as a small act of appreciation became a powerful tool to drive engagement and renewals. And it happened because we trusted the front line to make smart decisions within clearly defined boundaries. Their willingness to step in without hesitation turned a marketing test into a low-cost gesture that dramatically strengthened connections and deepened member loyalty.

Framework: The TRUST Loop for Frontline Innovation

How can you make this kind of innovation a repeatable, reliable process in your organization?

One way is to implement what I call the TRUST Loop, which is a simple framework to build autonomy with guardrails. Once you empower your employees, the loop repeats itself.

Close the TRUST Loop

- **T: Tell the *why*.** Before employees can act, they need to understand the reason behind the work. Why does customer or member retention matter? Why is attendance at educational programs critical? Clarity of purpose empowers smarter decisions.
- **R: Remove the red tape.** Audit your current approval processes. What decisions require a manager's sign-off? Could any of those be pushed down the chain of command with limits or thresholds (e.g., "Spend up to $250 without approval")?

- **U: Uncover patterns.** Encourage teams to document recurring complaints, inefficiencies, or customer questions. These patterns are gold mines of insight. They're often hiding in support tickets, hallway conversations, and help desk or chatbot logs.
- **S: Start small.** Allow and even encourage "micro-experiments." Test a solution with one location, one team, or one week. Document the result, share learnings, and decide if it's worth scaling or continuing to gather data and test.
- **T: Trust and Track.** Empower action and measure impact. Did the experiment reduce calls? Improve satisfaction? Drive attendance? Celebrate wins and learn from what didn't work. Innovation without measurement becomes guesswork.

PRACTICAL HOW-TO:
TURNING AUTONOMY INTO ACTION

Step 1: Choose a focus area. Pick a function where customer-facing interactions are frequent, such as the following:

- Membership services
- Front desk reception
- Call center support
- Healthcare practitioners who see patients
- Sales staff
- Administrative staff

Step 2: Set a boundary for action. Create a clear guideline like the following:

- Team members may issue up to $50 in credits without manager approval.
- If you can experiment or test a better way of handling a situation without additional funds, try it.

Step 3: Invite the first experiment. Run a seven-day challenge: "Fix one frustration. No approval needed. Just document what you did and why." Track the result and share with the team.

Step 4: Debrief and discuss. Hold a thirty-minute retrospective. Ask the following:

- *What worked?*
- *What didn't?*
- *What surprised you?*
- *Should we expand this?*

Step 5: Make it a habit. Build "mini pitches" into staff meetings. Create a shared innovation board where ideas get posted and tracked. Keep the barrier to testing low. The goal isn't perfection. It's learning.

Although I am a strong proponent of setting boundaries and trusting your frontline employees to explore creative ways to directly solve customer, patient, and client problems, I recognize that not all decisions can—or should—be made this way. Autonomy without clarity can create confusion, inconsistency, and risk. That's why it's critical to define the parameters within which decisions can be made. When organizations articulate clear decision rights, they don't restrict innovation; they focus it. Frontline innovation flourishes not in chaos, but within well-communicated constraints.

To do this effectively, organizations should consider tiered levels of decision-making authority and identify any bottlenecks that might prevent team members from trying new approaches. These layers might include micro fixes (low risk, like a new system for labeling cups), mid-level adjustments (moderate risk, such as altering a workflow or rescheduling appointments), and strategic shifts (high risk or high impact, like changing pricing or service models). By aligning actions to risk levels, employees gain clarity about when they can act independently and when to escalate.

Take, for example, a hotel chain that empowers front desk staff to offer up to $100 in perks or discounts to resolve guest complaints without needing manager approval. This small boundary gives staff a defined space in which to be responsive and personal, whether that's waiving a fee, upgrading a room, or offering free breakfast—while staying under budget and maintaining consistency across the brand. It's not a free-for-all. It's autonomy with purpose. And that's where real trust and real results begin.

Boundaries like these don't just reduce friction; they also empower action. When people know exactly how far they can go to fix a problem, they're more likely to step in with confidence. And when that clarity is paired with trust, innovation happens. I recently experienced this firsthand in a situation where the boundaries were clear, the front line was empowered, and the result turned a potentially frustrating experience into an unexpectedly impressive one.

The $800 Repair That Cost Me Nothing

I was staring at my brand-new MacBook Pro screen, watching dark horizontal and vertical lines spread like lightning from the impact point.

What had been a perfect display moments before was now carved up by these black bars that cut across everything, making half the screen unreadable. The actual crack in the glass was almost invisible, but those dark lines made it impossible to keep working on it. Twenty-seven days. I'd owned this laptop for exactly twenty-seven days, and somehow, I'd managed to crack the display.

I booked a Genius Bar appointment and walked into the Apple Store with a sense of dread.

That's when I met Dan. He greeted me, ran diagnostics, pulled up my purchase history, and examined the screen. He didn't say much at first. But he exuded a focused, competent calm.

Then he turned the screen toward me and said, "Here's the situation. If I send this out for repair through the standard process, it'll cost around $800. It's not covered under warranty because this is classified as accidental damage."

I braced myself. But then he paused.

"There's one other option."

He explained that because the MacBook was only twenty-seven days old, he could order the part and complete the repair in-store. It turns out that when repairs are done in-store on recently purchased devices, they fall under a different classification. One that, in this case, meant the entire repair would be free.

Same parts. Same outcome. Very different cost.

Dan hadn't broken protocol or pulled strings. He simply knew the system well enough to use a lesser-known process path—one that required no escalation, no manager override, and no "special exception." He used knowledge and judgment to do the right thing. And he changed the whole experience.

I walked in expecting a frustrating interaction. I walked out with my faith in frontline problem-solving restored.

Dan didn't invent a new policy. He didn't need to. What he did was something most employees never feel empowered to do: He navigated complexity with confidence and creativity.

This wasn't just customer service; it was innovation in action. A perfect example of what happens when you give frontline staff the following:

- The tools to understand the systems they work within.
- The autonomy to use their judgment.
- The trust that they'll prioritize the customer's experience as much as the company's bottom line.

That repair process probably saved Apple a long customer service call, a complaint, and potentially a lost customer (I had bought the laptop for $1,800 less than a month before, and the crack on the screen seemed to appear out of nowhere). Instead, it became a moment of unexpected delight—all because one employee understood that following a rule isn't the same as understanding its purpose.

Every organization has moments like this, forks in the road where the customer experience hinges not on the policy, but on how well an employee understands it. On whether they feel empowered to solve the problem, not just report it.

Dan didn't just fix a screen. He turned me into a lifelong MacBook Pro user who will go on to share this story with many people.

In that moment, he embodied what this chapter is all about: small acts of empowered problem-solving that deliver outsized impact.

Think about the invisible cracks in your organization—those places where the system technically works, but the experience falls flat. Where policies exist, but people are afraid to interpret them with humanity. Where decisions get bottlenecked, even when a solution is obvious.

Now ask yourself:

- *Who on my team interacts with customers, clients, members, or patients and can improvise solutions?*
- *Would they feel safe making that call? Do they understand the policies I have in place, and do they know where they can help customers within those boundaries?*
- *Have I made the boundaries of autonomy clear enough to invite action?*

Sometimes innovation isn't a big idea or a breakthrough. Sometimes it looks like a broken screen and someone who knows exactly how to fix it—and turn an anxious customer into an unofficial brand ambassador—without asking for permission.

That's the difference between procedure and ownership. Between a rigid process and a responsive one.

Implement This at Your Organization

1. **Look to your front lines.** Frontline employees are often the first to see recurring problems—and the first to imagine better solutions. They're not guessing or theorizing; they're living the experience in real time. Whether it's a nurse at a patient's bedside or a barista behind a counter, these employees understand the nuance, friction, and opportunity that leadership may never fully see. That makes their perspective essential, not optional, for meaningful innovation.

   But insight alone isn't enough. What sets the most agile organizations apart is that they don't just listen to frontline ideas; they empower people to act on them. When employees have the authority to run small tests, fix what's broken, and adapt systems in the moment, they can unlock a culture where solutions are born at the speed of experience. That's when trust becomes a competitive advantage.

2. **Start small, think big.** Every story in this chapter—from the letter "M" on a coffee cup to a PT joining a home care team—started small. There were no special budgets, no executive briefings, and no six-month strategy decks. Just a clear understanding of the problem, the freedom to act, and the courage to test something new. These micro-innovations didn't stay small for long. But they stayed rooted in simplicity and speed.

    Too often, organizations wait for permission, budget, or perfection. But big change doesn't require big beginnings. It requires action. Start by creating space for low-risk experiments. Protect time for reflection. Share results across teams. That's how small acts of courage become scalable systems of change.

3. **Create brave spaces through boundaries.** Empowerment doesn't mean an absence of rules; it means clarity about what's possible without asking for permission. When employees know their boundaries, they're more likely to feel bounded psychological safety, which helps them step into those constraints confidently. Whether it's a $250 budget to fix a customer issue or the autonomy to design a care plan, clear parameters remove the fog of uncertainty. And with that clarity comes speed, creativity, and ownership.

4. **Close the TRUST Loop.** *Tell the why, Remove red tape, Uncover patterns, Start small, and Trust and track*—offers a replicable way to embed autonomy throughout your organization. It's not about chaos. It's about disciplined freedom. That's what enables frontline employees to act with both courage and care—and ensures that innovation becomes a daily rhythm, not a top-down directive.

Empowering the front lines is a critical first step. But if innovation only happens in isolated pockets—when one barista, one nurse, or one member service rep goes above and beyond—you're still leaving too much to chance. The next leap isn't just more autonomy; it's building a system that encourages everyone to take more shots more often, while measuring whether they actually do.

In the final chapter, we'll explore what it takes to move from one-off success stories to a repeatable, scalable culture of experimentation. We'll look at how some organizations run dozens of micro-experiments at once, rather than betting big on one idea. We'll ask what it really means to measure shot-taking at the team and organizational level. Finally, we'll tackle the hard part: how to help risk-averse leaders and industries make the leap without losing their footing.

Not every shot is a smart one, so we'll also look at when not to experiment and how boundaries help us aim with intention. Because innovation isn't just about having more ideas; it's about building the system that makes trying them safe, strategic, and sustainable.

TIME TO THINK DIFFERENTLY

1. What recurring problems could your frontline team members solve if they had clearer boundaries and more autonomy?

2. How might your customer experience improve if those closest to your clients felt empowered to experiment with solutions?

3. What would change if you gave your team permission to spend a small amount (time or money) to "make things right" without asking permission?

CHAPTER 9

Leading a Shot-Taking Culture

In December 2023, I joined a group of thirty professional and amateur photographers on an expedition to Antarctica. I'd taken many photography trips to Africa before that, but this marked my first trip to a colder climate. Like that subsequent trip to the Arctic waters above Svalbard, Norway, this wasn't a sightseeing cruise; it was a photographic mission focused on capturing the raw, breathtaking beauty of one of the most remote regions on Earth. Our subjects included chinstrap and gentoo penguins, Weddell and leopard seals, seabirds like cormorants and petrels, and the dramatic, ice-sculpted landscapes that define the region.

With so many skilled photographers aboard, I knew I'd have a difficult time capturing a unique perspective or moment that no one else would get. Over the week, I took more than ten thousand photos, searching for something distinctive and memorable. Each day, I was the first photographer off the boat and the last one back. We faced a number of constraints due to an increase in avian flu and standard restrictions on where we could go and what we could do upon reaching the South Shetland Islands along the Antarctic Peninsula.

On the final day, before crossing back through the Drake Passage—infamous for its violent, forty-foot waves nicknamed the "Drake

Shake"—we expected to spend the day photographing the icy waters and snow-capped peaks.

Suddenly, a ship broadcast of the captain's voice interrupted our breakfast. The captain had spotted more than a dozen humpback whales nearby. They were bubble-net feeding, a sophisticated and rarely witnessed technique of synchronized hunting that involves a pod of whales spiraling upward to corral fish within a cylinder of bubbles—before lunging through the center to feed.

We had ten minutes to grab our red parkas, rubber boots, and camera gear before climbing into the Zodiac boats and moving closer to the action. The ship's photographer captured the scene from a drone while the rest of us, six people per boat, moved in to take our shots from sea level.

As we moved closer, I focused my camera on the whales and hit the shutter on my camera.

Because I can take up to thirty frames per second, I easily shot more than three thousand pictures. But as I scrolled through the shots, I didn't like what I saw. Some of the images featured other Zodiac boats in the background, filled with photographers all trying to capture the same shot. In others, the commotion of the feeding whales didn't translate into clear images or interesting compositions. Besides, it felt like all I could do was to replicate the same shots as everyone else in the boat.

Then, off in the distance, I spied a lone whale. It was breaching in apparent slow motion against the backdrop of snow-dusted mountains. The lighting was tough because I was shooting into a mixture of sun and fog which created a hazy, washed-out backdrop. Plus, the whale was more than three hundred meters away. But I realized that if I wanted to catch something different, I would have a better chance if I turned away from the feeding frenzy.

So, while others focused on the main spectacle, I turned my lens toward the solitary whale. Someone even told me I was "missing the shot." But I knew: Taking more shots isn't just about volume. It's about recognizing when to zig while others zag. It's about trusting your instincts to follow the story that no one else is paying attention to.

When we returned to the ship and shared our images, that photo—the peaceful whale tail, dripping with water as it dove back into the sea—immediately stood out among the bunch. Not because it was technically superior, but because it offered a different perspective. A choice. A risk.

That's what this final chapter is about: redefining what it means to take more shots. It's not just about doing more—taking more photographs or launching more projects—but about making intentional decisions to explore the unexpected. To stop following the same, predictable path and give yourself the freedom to explore new territory. Sometimes that means choosing the quiet, distant moment over the dramatic, obvious one. Sometimes it means stepping away from the crowd.

Because the real opportunity lies not just in taking *more* shots. It's about taking *better* risks.

The examples in this chapter show what can happen when leaders give frontline employees the freedom to solve a problem. Whether a barista with a marker, a nurse improvising real-time solutions, or a service rep with a sense of ownership, we've seen how small actions drive innovation when frontline teams feel empowered to act. But if we stop there—if those moments remain isolated wins—we risk missing the bigger opportunity: creating a culture where this kind of thinking isn't the exception; it's the expectation.

The real question isn't, *Can innovation happen on the front lines?* We've already seen that it can, given the opportunity. Instead, ask questions like the following:

- *How do we build a system where frontline innovation happens again and again—across roles, across teams, and across time?*
- *How do we create an environment where risk-taking isn't just allowed, but actively modeled, measured, and rewarded? Where creativity flourishes not in chaos, but within defined boundaries that make room for unscripted play?*

This chapter is about making that leap of scale: from one-off coffee cup changes to organization-wide practices. From trusting a nurse to test an idea to equipping an entire care system to run dozens of micro-experiments. From celebrating a single empowered employee to scaling the conditions that made that moment possible.

We've already discussed the power of frontline employees to take smart risks. To close out the book, we'll focus on what happens when CEOs do the same. Of course, taking more shots means increasing the likelihood of more failures. But when leaders track their own attempts and own their failures, risk-averse cultures shift. Everyone understands not just how to take a shot, but when not to. That is where innovative thrives.

Sometimes it all starts with a simple sheet of paper and a string of disappointments.

The Pink Paper That Started It All

When I was a freshman at Indiana University in Bloomington, I came back to my dorm room after a really difficult exam—one I'd pulled an all-nighter to prepare for—and felt like I'd failed, despite doing everything "right."

I dropped my backpack, slumped onto the lower bunk bed, and told my roommate, "This is definitely a *dammit* situation."

A week later, we got the exam results, and my biggest fear came true. I had earned a D on the exam, and I was now perilously close to failing my stats class. The following week, I applied to be a staff photographer at the student newspaper, the *Indiana Daily Student*, and was turned away. With slipping grades and without enough experience to join even the student-run paper, I felt lost in the woods, struggling to find my potential career path.

As I sat in my room, frustrated, I had an idea. I grabbed a piece of pink stationery and wrote, "This Is Definitely a Dammit Situation" across the top. Then, I listed both failures underneath. Rather than mulling these incidents repeatedly in my head, I'd list them out and talk them over with people I trusted.

Upon sharing these failures with two of my closest friends, Andrea and Catherine, they decided to add their own "Dammit Situations" to the list. Within an hour, we had compiled twenty. Finally, I taped the list to the outside of my dorm room door, along with a pen attached to a string.

Soon enough, people I didn't even know began contributing to the list. By the end of the school year, I had four sheets of paper taped to my door, documenting hundreds of failed student moments. Some were personal, such as failing to get a date for a dance or oversleeping and missing a class. Others related to career goals or dreams that seemed out of reach, like failed internship attempts or rejections from business school.

That list grew into more than just a catalog of bad days. It became a way to share failure publicly and safely. It also made room for empathy and problem-solving. My friends and I didn't always fix the issues, but we talked about them. We laughed, and we bonded.

Now, as I reflect back on that year, I realize that we also learned a lot. Many failures that seemed so enormous at the time had very little impact on our overall happiness and success that year. Plus, the list reminded us that we weren't alone. Luckily, I preserved both friendships from that year and the infamous list itself, which I'd slipped into one of my college scrapbooks. Recently, after chatting with Andrea, I dug it out of a box in the basement.

I kept that list because it represents something I've carried with me into every job—and now as the CEO of my own company: the belief that failure doesn't have to be hidden. In fact, naming failures, mistakes, and disappointments might be the first step toward building a culture where it's safe to take more shots. That's what this chapter is about: the systems, behaviors, and mindset shifts that make risk-taking not just tolerated, but expected.

Welcome to the architecture of a shot-taking culture.

That pink piece of paper taught me that when people feel safe to share a failure, they're more willing to take the next shot. But it's not just about safety at the peer level; it's also about modeling this behavior from the top. If leaders don't talk about their own missteps, no one else will feel comfortable doing it.

That's why I've always admired the way Ed Catmull, co-founder of Pixar, talked openly about failure—not just as a necessary part of the creative process, but also as a leadership responsibility. I was recently reminded of his take on failure while listening the expanded audio version of his book, *Creativity, Inc.*

Catmull understood that failure wasn't something to be avoided; it was something to be managed, studied, and, most importantly, shared. In *Creativity, Inc.*, he describes a moment when a movie in development called *Newt* wasn't working.[1] The story felt disjointed, the characters fell flat, and despite a talented team, the project stalled. So, they shelved it and turned their attention elsewhere. More importantly, they openly shared why it was shelved:

1. Catmull couldn't make either the storyline or the characters resonate emotionally, a core principle for Pixar. The plot—that the last two remaining endangered blue-footed newts had

to couple up, despite hating each other, in order to save their species—felt forced.

2. A similar animated film project in development by another studio also focused on rare, endangered animals. The overlap made *Newt* feel less original.

3. Although they tried to reboot the project with new creative leads, exploring a different storyline, the story and characters just didn't evolve.

Eventually, the decision was made to pull the plug and redirect efforts into other projects, including *Inside Out*. Importantly, Catmull didn't treat the failed project as a black mark on the organization's record. He treated it as part of the job.

"Failure isn't a necessary evil," he wrote. "It's a necessary consequence of doing something new."[2] At Pixar, leaders didn't just accept the failure; they openly talked about it at team-wide meetings. They dissected and examined what worked and what didn't. Above all, they modeled what it looked like to move forward without shame. I believe this was their version of that pink sheet paper titled "This Is Definitely a Dammit Situation."

The truth is that no one *likes* to fail. No one wants to put an enormous amount of effort into something that produces no results. These are still "Dammit Situations." However, if you can acknowledge that these situations can also lead to breakthroughs, innovations, or better solutions, then you create a culture that embraces creative risk and innovates as a matter of course.

That kind of top-down modeling makes risk-taking possible at scale. If a leader can stand up and say, "Here's what I tried, here's what didn't work, and here's what I learned," it invites others to do the same. It normalizes experimentation and shifts the culture from one that rewards only outcomes to one that values the process of trying.

Knowing When to Walk Away

Organizations sometimes fall into the trap of keeping projects on life support long after they've outlived their purpose or failed to deliver results. It usually starts with good intentions. Perhaps a team embraces the idea of "taking more shots" and experiments with launching a few new products, programs, or initiatives. But when one of those shots misses the mark, instead of shutting it down and learning from it, the organization keeps it alive. The project lingers, draining time, money, and energy, even when it's clear it will never meet its original goals.

There are a few reasons why this happens. Sometimes a project becomes someone's "pet," protected by a senior leader or volunteer who originally championed the idea. This is especially common in associations, where initiatives may be tied to past board members or committees, so people hesitate to question them out of loyalty or fear of offending someone. I saw this firsthand many years ago while working at an association that hosted a large annual event benefiting a local nonprofit. When I joined the organization, no one could recall why the nonprofit had been chosen, who initiated the idea, or how it aligned with the association mission. Despite this lack of clear strategy, significant staff time and resources were dedicated to producing the event each year.

After managing the event my first year, I began openly questioning whether or not it still served our goals—and whether we could redirect the proceeds to our own foundation instead. Some people on the team seemed nervous about how members might react. *Would they be disappointed? Would they expect the tradition to continue?*

Others welcomed the change. They knew how much time and capital we annually funneled into the event, and the relatively low return on investment to the association. Ultimately, I made the decision to retire the event. We replaced it with a new experience that still brought members together in a meaningful way, but this time the proceeds supported our own mission. Killing the project opened the door to a better, more strategic initiative. It also sent a powerful signal that we were willing to evolve, not just maintain tradition for tradition's sake.

Projects like that event at my former association are sometimes called *zombies*. They are programs, products, projects, and processes that should be dead—but somehow live on. They consume time, resources, and attention without delivering meaningful value. Whether a lackluster movie idea or a misaligned event, zombies often drag themselves along simply out of inertia, because no one wants to take the trouble to kill them. Characteristics of *zombie* projects include the following:

- no longer aligned with strategic priorities
- no longer owned or championed by specific leaders or team members
- still on life support due to *sunk cost bias* ("we've already spent so much on it")
- carrying on out of habit, politics, or fear of backlash
- draining resources away from other projects

How to Identify and Kill the Zombies

Step 1: Take inventory. Make a list of current projects, initiatives, or programs currently being developed and supported. These could be legacy programs, tech tools or platforms, events, or products with declining sales, interest, or relevancy to your target audience.

Step 2: Do a health review. For each item, answer the following questions with a coding system (Red = likely a zombie, Yellow = under review, Green = alive and well):

- *What problem was the program, product, or service meant to solve?*
- *Does that problem still exist?*
- *Is this the best or most viable solution to the problem?*
- *When was the last time it provided meaningful results?*
- *Does it offer a solution that cannot be found in the current market?*
  Do any competitors offer a better solution?
- *What resources, time, money, or people does it consume?*
- *Does anyone own or champion it as a viable solution?*
- *Would anyone notice or care if it disappeared?*

Step 3: Reassess and release. Review the Red/Yellow items and for each one, ask the following:

- *What's stopping us from letting go?*
- *Are we keeping it alive out of habit, fear, or politics?*
- *Could we redirect the resources to another initiative that will likely have a higher impact?*

Step 4: Take action. For each zombie you identify, be ruthless. Kill the project and reassign resources toward something that solves a core customer problem more aligned with your strategy and strengths. If people push back, share the metrics you used to assess the viability and impact of the program, product, or service. Ask colleagues where they might direct resources now that they've been freed up and are no longer supporting the zombie project.

Window of Opportunity

When a new CEO or leader joins an organization, there's often a brief but powerful window of opportunity to reset the culture—to signal that things can and will be different, starting now. One of the most important cultural shifts a leader can spark is encouraging people to take more shots: to experiment, test ideas, and speak up without fear of failure. But fostering that kind of environment takes more than a motivational speech. It requires clear modeling, permission structures, and a consistent message that learning and progress matter more than perfection.

One of the first things a new leader can do is ask, "What are we *not* trying—and *why*?" This question alone can surface hidden fears, approval bottlenecks, and outdated assumptions that stifle innovation. It also communicates curiosity rather than blame. Leaders should reward the act of trying, not just the outcomes. That might mean spotlighting a failed initiative in a team meeting and applauding the effort or sharing what was learned from a miss just as openly as a win. Over time, this approach normalizes risk-taking and rewires the team's relationship with failure.

A few years ago, I worked with a new CEO who inherited a risk-averse culture where employees rarely shared new ideas in meetings. On her first week, she set up "idea office hours" and encouraged anyone, regardless of title, to pitch something new—no slides, no budget asks, just the idea. One of the ideas came from a young professional who suggested turning a newsletter expert profile into a live Q&A series with rotating experts. It was easy to test and offered a clearer connection to engagement. The initial plan was to host one Q&A live webinar every other month to gauge interest and participation. After the projected proved to be an immediate success (based on the high number of individuals who registered for the event), the organization expanded it to once a month and kept a wait-list of experts eager to participate.

As culture evolves, leaders should create visible systems to support experimentation. This might include "pilot and measure" frameworks, micro-grants for internal initiatives, or rapid debrief sessions after launches. These structures reinforce that experimentation shouldn't be haphazard or unplanned, but rather strategic. They also show how risk-taking can be integrating seamlessly into normal workflow, not just something people do "on the side" if they have extra time or political capital to spare.

Ultimately, creating a culture where people take more shots isn't about hitting some quota on taking random big risks; it's about removing the obstacles that make taking chances less risky. A new leader faces a unique chance to reset those conditions—not by demanding innovation, but by designing a workplace where trying something new feels both possible and safe.

Of course, creating a culture where people take more shots isn't only the domain of new leaders; it's just as critical—and just as possible—for those who've been in their roles for years. In fact, long-tenured leaders may have an even greater opportunity to model change because they already hold the trust and credibility of their teams. What matters most is signaling a shift—showing that from this point forward, experimentation is not just accepted but expected.

For existing leaders, the first step is often acknowledging the past. A simple statement like, "We've been cautious—and for good reasons, at times—but now it's time to stretch," can go a long way. It validates the previous culture without being bound by it. Leaders who've been in place for a while also have access to institutional knowledge, which can be a strength. They know where the bottlenecks lie, where ideas die, and which quiet innovators have been holding back. If you're that veteran leader, use your knowledge to clear the path.

Modeling risk-taking often starts by owning your own missteps. Eric O'Connor, chief innovation officer at the American Association of Nurse Anesthesiology (AANA), shared a story that's become part of his team's cultural DNA. Early in his tenure, he helped create a high-profile video meant to tell member stories, which staff and focus groups had approved and encouraged.

But when the video was released publicly, it went viral for all the wrong reasons. Members hated it. Rather than burying the failure, Eric used it as a teaching moment. He continues to tell the story, often making fun of himself in meetings, to signal to his team that it's okay to fail, especially if you're trying something bold. That one moment, he said, helped give others permission to take risks, even on a big stage. It's now part of the culture: a shared memory that fosters courage instead of caution.

Alongside humility and storytelling, leaders—new or seasoned—can create systems that embed experimentation into everyday work. Instead of confining innovation to a department or a brainstorming retreat, they can normalize pilot projects, cross-functional teams, and rapid feedback loops. One effective strategy involves bringing diverse voices together early in a project—from junior staff to designers to end users—and creating space for input before decisions get locked in. As Eric put it, the creative team at AANA used to be brought in at the end to "pretty things up." Now they're involved from the start, helping to strategically shape projects and turning them into experiences that resonate more deeply with members.

Ultimately, cultures of innovation aren't built by demanding boldness; they're built by reducing the fear that comes with trying something new. That starts with leaders willing to take the first shot, miss publicly, and still come back with confidence and curiosity. Whether you're new to your role or have been there for decades, the ability to change your culture doesn't depend on tenure. It depends on trust, example, and a steady drumbeat of permission to try.

How to Build a Shot-Taking Culture

1. **Name the boundaries and the playground.** Boundaries reduce ambiguity and increase creativity. When everyone understands

the rules, they feel safe to experiment. Clarify what's fixed and what's flexible. Examples of fixed boundaries may include technology platform, target audience, and the product itself, but how it gets sold may be flexible. Other boundaries may include how much money or time can be spent to test a solution.

2. **Reward the tries, not just the wins.** Publicly acknowledge people who took a thoughtful risk, even if the results didn't pan out. Make it clear that effort, curiosity, and learning are just as valuable as results. Consider offering a "First Shot" award to someone on the staff who suggests a potentially realistic new idea worth trying—regardless of the outcome.

3. **Embrace the misses.** Leaders should regularly share the times they tried and failed. It's easier for the team to take a shot when they know, with full certainty, that the organization will celebrate both wins and losses, as long as they provide insights into what works and what doesn't. When a leader talks openly about a failed idea, it gives everyone the permission to discuss missteps. This vulnerability builds trust and fuels innovation.

4. **Track shot attempts, not just conversions.** If you only measure success, you'll only analyze safe bets. Track how many new ideas were tested and share that data too. When teams see that trying matters as much as winning, they become more willing to act.

5. **Create a safety net.** Let teams know where they can fail without fear of penalty. Define zones of freedom, like, "You can test anything under $1,000," or "Try it with one client or department first." This clarity builds confidence and reduces paralysis.

When people know the guardrails, they're more likely to explore within them.

6. **Build debriefing into the workflow.** Make debriefs a routine part of every project. They should be short, honest, and blame-free. The goal isn't to critique performance—it's to extract insights. Ask, *What worked? What didn't? What surprised us? What would we change next time?* When teams know they'll reflect later on the process and results, they pay more attention to learning in real time.

7. **Celebrate the "Pink Paper" moments.** Encourage public acknowledgment of failure. As a leader, start with your own. Create a digital or physical "Dammit Board" where team members can post something they tried but didn't work. This turns failure into a collective team-building experience, not an isolating one. Humor and empathy always help.

8. **Invite diverse voices early.** Bring in frontline staff, junior team members, and cross-functional partners at the beginning stages of idea development. Innovation thrives when all voices are heard. This can reduce groupthink and help identify blind spots.

9. **De-zombify your projects regularly.** Most organizations have some zombies shuffling around. Schedule biannual "zombie audits" to identify and retire these projects. Use criteria like relevance, ownership, ROI, and strategic alignment. Keep in mind that not every organization will identify zombies at every audit, especially if they already use a process to evaluate the viability, relevance, and value of their product portfolio.

10. **Make shot-taking a leadership KPI (key performance indicator).** Include experimentation and learning in leadership evaluations. Ask, *How many pilots did your team launch? What did you learn from something that didn't work? Who on your team took a bold risk?* This reinforces that innovation is core to leadership. What gets measured gets encouraged.

We've seen what happens when an organization moves from one-off events to a sustained shot-taking culture. A culture where people across all levels are not just allowed to take risks, but are expected and actively encouraged to experiment and try new things. Where both creativity and innovation occur within the defined boundaries, because within that's where there's room to play.

But here's the thing: This isn't just about creating more brainstorming sessions or launching one new initiative. It's about reimagining the mechanism for how new ideas surface and how they get tested, evaluated, celebrated, and used as a strategy for growth. Leaders identify the boundaries and reward attempts. They publicly acknowledge their own failures and share what they've learned. They model this behavior.

Culture cascades from the top. If leaders don't demonstrate risk-taking, no one else will feel safe enough to try. That's why it matters when a CEO or chief innovation officer tells the story of a failed initiative. It's why it matters when a leader retires an ineffective program, or simply just walks in and asks, "What are we not trying and why?"

These actions signal that this is a place where anyone can take more shots and everyone's voice is valued. Where failure is expected, because it means the organization is trying something new—not stagnating in some comfort zone that may reduce your organization's relevance, impact, or growth.

Admittedly, my pink sheet of paper back in college wasn't born from strategy. It was born from frustration, vulnerability, and a desire to not carry my failures alone. What started as a way to manage a personal disappointment became a shared experience and an opportunity to bond, learn, and grow—together. That, too, is the essence of a shot-taking culture: one where failure isn't hidden but shared. Where disappointment isn't shameful but human. And where the next shot is always possible because people believe they are allowed to take it.

The future belongs to the organizations that build this kind of culture, where trying is celebrated as a core part of the work.

As I close this chapter and this book, consider the following questions: *What is your version of the pink sheet? What boundaries can you name? What systems can you shape? Finally, what will you do to ensure the people you lead know they have permission to take more shots?*

Because when trying becomes the expectation—not the exception—that's where it's safe to really play. And that's where innovation begins.

TIME TO THINK DIFFERENTLY

1. What would you be willing to try if you knew your organization celebrated both bold attempts and valuable failures?
2. How could you model the risk-taking behavior you want to see throughout your team?
3. What "zombie projects" in your organization need to be retired to make room for fresh experimentation?

CONCLUSION

"What do you do for work?"

It's a question I'm asked nearly every day—on airplanes, on the tennis court, and at events—because I am constantly meeting new people. The answer is both simple and complicated.

I help individuals and teams innovate.

When I'm asked to give an example or share a story, I often tell people about the playground experiment conducted by the landscape architect, Tatiana Zakharova-Goodman, and her desire to explore how boundaries affect how children play. Those kids didn't need more space to explore; they just needed to know where the edges lay—how far they could go and still feel safe.

Staying on the playground restricted their play to the same old slides, swings, and merry-go-round they've always known. The same ups and downs. The same back-and-forth. The same endless, predictable loops. They moved in ways dictated by past constructs and old equipment and by uncertainty around what *else* could be possible.

Once they knew where the fences were, their playground got bigger, and they became more creative in their play. They stretched the limits of their imagination when their play was left unscripted—within a few clearly defined constraints.

We often hear the phrase "think outside the box" tossed around like it's the only path to innovation. But here's the truth: Outside-the-box thinking is only effective when you appreciate the full potential of what's inside the box to begin with. Creativity flourishes not from chaos, but from leveraging the structures, resources, and strategic limitations you're already working within. It's hard to bend rules if no one knows what the rules are in the first place.

This is the same opportunity you have as a leader.

You don't need to "tear down fences" or "push beyond boundaries" to give your teams endless freedom to innovate. In fact, that level of freedom can lead either to paralysis, or to dispersed efforts with little strategy or ROI. If you want a more creative "sandbox" culture, stop scattering sand around. Get clear about the boundaries and try thinking *inside* the box from time to time.

A well-designed sandbox is the perfect metaphor. It's not infinite, but it is full of possibility. The edges aren't there to restrict play— they're there to concentrate it. A defined space invites experimentation because it removes the fear of unintended consequences. Inside the sandbox, people know what tools they have, how far they can go, and what happens if they spill a little sand. That's bounded psychological safety. It says, "Take risks—but here's how we do that safely, together."

Your team doesn't need (or want) unlimited resources or wide-open spaces. What they need is a culture that gets clear on *boundaries*, listens (and responds) to every *voice*, and gives *permission* to try.

Walls and fences create clarity: about where the organization is going, where its priorities lie, and what risks can be taken. Clarity about who gets to weigh in and when it's time to move on from a project that no longer produces results or aligns with the mission.

Creativity doesn't come from unlimited freedom but from structure that leaves room for play.

If you've read this far, chances are, you're ready to take more shots yourself to help your organization become more innovative and adaptive to a changing environment. You want to spark real innovation that isn't a reaction to the latest trend. Something original and creative, relevant and *real*, born from a culture where everyone has a voice and new ideas can flourish.

This kind of culture doesn't happen by accident. It's designed.

So, how do you design a culture that sets clear boundaries, listens to every voice, and gives permission to try? How do you establish those fences and sandbox walls that spark creative play, teamwork, and growth?

Setting boundaries: Clarify priorities, standards, and expectations. Make them visible, not vague. Tell people what your organization values most and how you allocate time, attention, and resources. In these ways, you can bake experimentation right into the DNA of your organization.

Elevating voices: Share and solicit ideas and experimentation at every level. Ask better questions from team members who work at the front lines, in middle management, and across departments. Seek out feedback—and act on it.

Giving permission to try: Make experimentation safe and visible. Reward learning, not just successes. Regularly revisit and either reform or discard old, outdated models. Recognize and share micro-wins and micro-losses. Model learning from, talking about—even celebrating— failure, right from the top.

Of course, sometimes the box is too small. Sometimes the sandbox needs expansion, or the fence needs to move. The key is intentionality. Leaders who excel at innovation don't default to tearing things down. They examine the edges, test their flexibility, and expand the perimeter with purpose. They give teams enough structure to feel safe and enough freedom to be bold. The innovation sweet spot lies at that intersection.

These practices fuel true risk-taking and cultivate a shot-taking culture. Because they build a sense of trust, ownership, and confidence.

It's time to look at your own playground and ask yourself the following:

- *Where are the fences? Are they clear? Are they strategic? Are they left over from a previous era?*
- *Who gets to play? Is it always the same voices? Are we opening up opportunities for other voices to be heard and contribute?*
- *When was the last time we rewarded an experiment—even one that didn't succeed?*

Asking these questions—within your leadership team, your board of directors, your volunteer leaders, and your teams—is the first step toward building an organization where innovation is built into the culture.

I've learned a lot from working with hundreds of organizations and analyzing more than one million data points on workforce challenges over two decades. Mainly, that innovation doesn't just happen. It's not about just luck or the size of your budget. It's not about giving your team free rein to do anything and everything (which is not possible). It's about creating a structure that nourishes ideas and combines bounded psychological safety and clarity around constraints.

This book offers ideas, research, case studies, and tools. But ultimately, it's your action that matters. The real work begins when you take these ideas and apply them: to your next meeting, your next decision, your next team conversation.

Innovation takes root when teams know where the boundaries lie; they feel safe, trusted, and valued; and they know they have the permission to try.

The fence was never just about reining the kids in. It was also about showing them how far they could go. Likewise, the sandbox walls are not about restricting resources but about maximizing the creative potential of what's right in front of you. What if your job as a leader isn't to remove all fences and walls but to provide the clarity needed to show your team how far they can go—how many shots they can take—and the freedom and resources to experiment?

How big is your playground?

It's yours to define—to unlock the hidden power of thinking inside the box and create space for you, your team, and your organization to take more shots.

ENDNOTES

Introduction

1 Tatiana Zakharova-Goodman, *Play/Grounding: Intersection of Pedagogy and Design of Outdoor ECE Play Spaces*, Climate Action Childhood Network, 2021. Informal study exploring how playground fences influence children's play and reflect educational and political values.

Chapter 1

1 The frigid temperature at which both Fahrenheit and Celsius metrics align.
2 *The Next Great Era of Cinema: A Special Report*, Cinema United, March 27, 2025, https://cinemaunited.org/wp-content/uploads/2025/03/The-Next-Great-Era-of-Cinema-Report-March-2025-1.pdf Yahoo+10Cinema United+10Cinema United+10.
3 Cinema United, *The Next Great Era of Cinema: A Special Report.*
4 CJ 4DPLEX. "CJ 4DPLEX and Regal Open the World's Largest 4DX Auditorium in Times Square." *CJ ENM Newsroom*, March 6 2024.
5 Cinema United, *The Next Great Era of Cinema: A Special Report.*
6 David Darr, "Giving Viewers What They Want," *New York Times*, June 23, 2013, https://www.nytimes.com/2013/06/23/magazine/netflix-and-the-future-of-television.html.
7 Ashley Rodriguez, "Netflix Divides Its 93 Million Users Around the World into 1,300 'Taste Communities,'" *Quartz*, last updated July 21, 2022, https://qz.com/939195/netflix-nflx-divides-its-93-million-users-around-the-world-not-by-geography-but-into-1300-taste-communities.
8 David Carr, "The Queen's Gambit and the Netflix Way," *New York Times*, October 23, 2020, https://www.nytimes.com/2020/10/23/arts/television/queens-gambit-netflix.html.
9 Rodriguez, "Netflix Divides."

10 Ted Sarandos, quoted in John Koblin, "Netflix Is Not a Public Utility," *New York Times*, July 19, 2019.

11 Shonda Rhimes, "The Answer Was Always Just, 'Yes, Yes, Yes,'" *Decider*, April 29, 2024.

Chapter 2

1 On, "The Roger," lifestyle sneaker, debuted July 2020; "The Roger Pro," performance court shoe, introduced 2021, in collaboration with Roger Federer as investor, On AG.[1]

2 "Advantage On! World No. 1 & 3-time Grand Slam Champion Iga Świątek and Rising Star Ben Shelton Join On as It Expands Its Presence in Professional Tennis," On, March 20, 2023.

3 "Zendaya and On Announce Multi-Year Partnership Focused on Movement and Storytelling," On, June 6, 2024.

4 "About Betty," Betty.ai, accessed June 2025. Betty is named after Betty Holberton ... ENIAC ... world's first general purpose electronic computer.

Chapter 3

1 Association Forum, "Association Professionals Through the Ages," July 26, 2008, YouTube, https://www.youtube.com/watch?v=mKSvgmpVJFk.

2 In August 2022, the White House Office of Science and Technology Policy issued a memorandum directing all federal agencies to ensure that publicly funded research is made freely and immediately available to the public by the end of 2025. See: Office of Science and Technology Policy, "Ensuring Free, Immediate, and Equitable Access to Federally Funded Research," 2022, https://www.whitehouse.gov/ostp/news-updates/2022/08/25/ensuring-free-immediate-and-equitable-access-to-federally-funded-research/.

3 "Books Unbanned: A National Campaign to Protect the Freedom to Read," Brooklyn Public Library, 2022, https://www.bklynlibrary.org/books-unbanned.

4 Sam Ritchie, Co-founder, FrogRocket Labs, https://www.linkedin.com/in/sritchie09/.

5 "Interaction Design Specialization," University of California, San Diego, Coursera, https://www.coursera.org/specializations/interaction-design.

6 Alex Glushenkov, "Apple Design Principles: A Legacy of Innovation, Elegance and Vision," Medium, January 24, 2023, https://medium.com/@alexglushenkov/apple-design-principles-a-legacy-of-innovation-elegance-and-vision-6d1f99a4331b.

Chapter 4

1 Alex Glushenkov, "Apple Design Principles: A Legacy of Innovation, Elegance and Vision," Medium, January 24, 2023, https://medium.com/@alexglushenkov/apple-design-principles-a-legacy-of-innovation-elegance-and-vision-6d1f99a4331b.

2 Felix Oberholzer-Gee and Adi Ignatius, "How to Reinvent a Consumer Brand," *HBR IdeaCast*, August 15, 2023, Harvard Business Review, https://hbr.org/podcast/2023/08/how-to-reinvent-a-consumer-brand.

3 Terence Reilly, interview by Bob Lefsetz, *The Bob Lefsetz Podcast*, podcast audio, March 23, 2023, https://www.iheart.com/podcast/1119-the-bob-lefsetz-podcast-30717378/episode/terence-reilly-111434064/.

4 The Buy Guide founders, with backing from Stanley, placed a wholesale order of five thousand Stanley Quencher cups, which sold out in five days; a subsequent five-thousand-unit reorder sold out in just one hour.

5 Jessica Testa, "How the Stanley Quencher Became the Tumbler of Choice," *New York Times*, July 18, 2023, https://www.nytimes.com/2023/07/18/style/stanley-quenchers.html.

6 Ann Zimmerman, "How Ron Johnson Misjudged J.C. Penney's Shoppers," *Wall Street Journal*, April 9, 2013, https://www.wsj.com/articles/SB10001424127887323646604578400771399907840.

Chapter 5

1 Amy C. Edmondson, *The Fearless Organization: Creating Psychological Safety in the Workplace for Learning, Innovation, and Growth* (Wiley, 2019), 15.

2 Intuit Inc., "Intuit's Culture of Experimentation and Failure Awards," *Harvard Business Review*, accessed June 21, 2025, https://hbr.org/2021/01/intuits-culture-of-experimentation-and-failure-awards.

3 Scott Cook, quoted in Eric Ries, *The Startup Way: How Modern Companies Use Entrepreneurial Management to Transform Culture and Drive Long-Term Growth* (Currency, 2017), 75.

4 Amy C. Edmondson, *Right Kind of Wrong: The Science of Failing Well* (Atria Books, 2023), 13.

5 David Marx, *Patient Safety and the "Just Culture": A Primer for Health Care Executives* (Columbia University, 2001), https://psnet.ahrq.gov/sites/default/files/just%20culture%20primer.pdf.

6 NASA, *Aviation Safety Reporting System: Program Briefing* (NASA Ames Research Center, 2021), https://asrs.arc.nasa.gov/docs/ASRS_ProgramBriefing.pdf.

7 "Battle Motors Expands Ohio Facility and Debuts Smart Cab," *Truck News*, October 6, 2022, https://www.trucknews.com/equipment/battle-motors-expands-ohio-facility-and-debuts-smart-cab/1003161370/.

Chapter 6

1   David Robertson and Bill Breen, *Brick by Brick: How LEGO Rewrote the Rules of Innovation and Conquered the Global Toy Industry* (Crown Business, 2013).
2   Guijie Qi et al., "How Does User Social Network Improve Innovation Outcomes on a Virtual Innovation Platform?: Evidence from LEGO Ideas Platform," *Journal of Global Information Management* 29, no. 3 (April 30, 2021): 188–211.
3   *2014 ACC Global Work-Life Balance Report: Executive Summary*, Association of Corporate Counsel, 2014, Washington, DC, https://www.acc.com/resource-library/2014-acc-global-work-life-balance-report.

Chapter 7

1   "How Amazon Defines and Operationalizes a Day 1 Culture," AWS Executive Insights, https://aws.amazon.com/executive-insights/content/how-amazon-defines-and-operationalizes-a-day-1-culture/.
2   Jeff Bezos, *2016 Amazon Shareholder Letter* (Amazon.com, Inc., 2016), https://s2.q4cdn.com/299287126/files/doc_financials/annual/Amazon_Shareholder_Letter.pdf.
3   "How Jeff Bezos Skyrocketed Amazon's Growth with a 'Day 1' Mindset," *CSQ*, August 2020, https://csq.com/2020/08/how-jeff-bezos-skyrocketed-amazons-growth-with-a-day-1-mindset/.

Chapter 8

1   KPMG, *Evaluation of the Buurtzorg Nederland Model of Nursing Care*, 2012, https://assets.kpmg.com/content/dam/kpmg/pdf/2012/10/kpmg-buurtzorg-report.pdf.

Chapter 9

1   Ed Catmull and Amy Wallace, *Creativity, Inc.: Overcoming the Unseen Forces That Stand in the Way of True Inspiration* (Random House, 2014).
2   Ed Catmull and Amy Wallace, *Creativity, Inc.: Overcoming the Unseen Forces That Stand in the Way of True Inspiration* (Random House, 2014), 109.

ACKNOWLEDGMENTS

I'm deeply grateful to the incredible individuals who generously shared their time, insights, and experiences during the writing of this book. Your stories, candor, and creativity brought these ideas to life. Thank you to Elena Gerstman, Gary LaBranche, Eric O'Connor, Lou DiGioia, Beth Surmont, Kelleigh Shankel, Christina Lewellen, Troy Henikoff, Halee Fischer-Wright, Rob Barnes, Brad Feld, Dan Chuparkoff, and Sam Ritchie for letting me peek behind the curtain and learn from your failures, your breakthroughs, and your belief in what's possible.

ABOUT THE AUTHOR

No matter the industry, organizations are all asking the same question: "How do we stay relevant, innovative, and connected to the people we serve?" Sheri Jacobs has spent her career helping organizations answer that question. She's a best-selling author, entrepreneur, and data-driven strategist who has worked with more than three hundred organizations, startups, and Fortune 500 companies to uncover what truly drives engagement, loyalty, and growth.

As the founder of Avenue M, Sheri has collected over a million data points across industries—from healthcare and education to finance, technology, and beyond—helping organizations turn insights into action. She's also the author of three best-selling books, including *Pivot Point: Reshaping Your Business When It Matters Most*, a guide for organizations navigating change and transformation. But her perspective isn't just shaped by data—it's enriched by her creativity and passion. She's an award-winning wildlife photographer who has traveled to all seven continents, capturing moments from polar bears in the Arctic to elephants in Zambia.